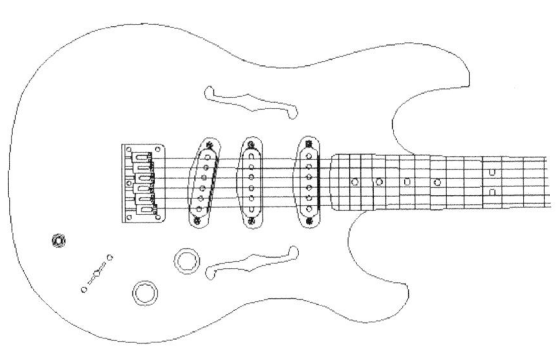

How to Make Rees S-Style Semi-Acoustic Guitars

First Edition
Copyright 2020 Clive M. Rees

Revision 1.02

Book Cover Back

This book describes how you, at home, can fairly easily make a professional quality guitar, at an attractive low cost. This is a performance guitar, that is both fully electric, and fully acoustic, and is of high musical quality. Only a small set of tools are needed to build it. These new Rees Semi-Acoustic guitars are innovative, patent pending, registered designs. They are great for loud electric stage performance; and for quiet acoustic playing at home.

You can find video reviews and demonstrations of these innovative guitars on Youtube. Search for Youtube Channel:

CliveRees MakingGuitarBooks

or click on the link above.

See my web-site: historical, and new:

www.rees-electric-guitars.com

Click on this to see my website, which supports these books with the latest info of:

Reviews and Demos of these Guitars.
Directory of Suppliers of Woods, Parts, and Tools to make these Guitars.
Book Revision History, including a list of any errors found in drawings or text.

The historic large part of the website shows my guitar making work, throughout the past 14 years.

1) Introduction

Clive Rees "retired" when 65yrs young in 2018, following a successful 12 year career of designing and making professional custom electric guitars and basses. During that era, he dabbled in the design of semi-acoustic guitars.

He has continued to apply his creative energies to invent a new construction for semi-acoustic guitars, which has louder acoustic performance, with more expressive electric performance.

Early versions of these "Pat. Pend." Rees semi-acoustic guitars had large expensive bodies of hardwood, with fine sitka spruce front soundboards, of the quality that are used on the very best acoustic guitars of this world. They sounded great acoustically, and electrically. They were very good to play, but rather big and heavy, and inevitably expensive to make.

Following some scientific analysis of the instrument vibrations, during a visit to the University of Cambridge Engineering Department, Clive discovered a game-changing use of different wood. Newly available birch plywood might be used. This can now be very thin for the soundboard, or of various standard thicknesses for the body. Birch plywood is manufactured to higher quality standards than traditional plywoods, and is of a moderate cost when compared to hardwoods. Traditional plywoods were never thin enough to make a great soundboard, and so got a bad reputation in acoustic guitars. However, if thinner stronger birch plywood is combined with some innovative strutting, it becomes possible to construct a great sounding small front soundboard.

These Rees semi-acoustic guitars are now the same size as common solid body electric guitars, which makes them very light, and comfortable to play. The fully developed soundboard now, is just as good, for a fraction of the cost of the exotic spruce tone-wood soundboard. This, together with the Pat. Pend. Internal bridge mechanism, makes a family of very exciting versatile guitars.

Now Clive is writing, and selling, books which describe how you can make these new superior guitar designs at home, with a small number of tools. Clive fully explains how to make these guitars, with many step-by-step photographs.

His complete detailed, accurately dimensioned, technical drawings are included in every book, in both mm and inches.

Table of Contents

    Book Cover Back..2

1) Introduction..3

    1.1) Quick and Easy to Make...12

    1.2) Innovative Pat. Pend. Design..12

    1.3) Industry Standard Neck Joint...13

    1.4) Playing Acoustic..13

    1.5) Playing Electric..13

    1.6) About the Author..14

2) Various Guitar Construction Methods..15

    2.1) Traditional Spanish Guitars – difficulty 10...15

    2.2) Traditional Flat-top Steel String Guitars – difficulty 12.......................15

    2.3) Traditional F-Hole Arch-top Guitars – difficulty 20.............................15

    2.4) Traditional Solid Electric Guitars – difficulty 5....................................16

    2.5) Rees Semi-Acoustic Guitars – difficulty 3...16

3) Construction of the Rees Semi-Acoustic..17

    3.1) The Laminated Body...17

    3.2) Typical Body Centre Cross-Section in Inches.......................................19

    3.3) Typical Body Centre Cross-Section in Metric......................................20

    3.4) The Soundboard with Struts..21

    3.5) The Pat. Pend. Inside of the Bridge...23

4) Parts and Materials...24

4.1) Materials to Make This Guitar...24

4.2) Parts to Make This Guitar:..28

5) Tools..30

5.1) Drilling Tools..30

5.2) Hand Coping Saw..31

5.3) Optional Powered Scroll Saw...32

5.4) Other Essential Tools..33

5.4) Optional Useful Tools...35

6) How to Use Your Tools with Best Skill...36

6.1) How to Mark Out Wood...36

6.2) How to Drill Holes Accurately..36

6.3) Sawing All the Curves..37

6.4) How to Use a Coping Saw..38

6.5) How to Use a Power Scroll Saw..40

6.6) How to Shape Wood...41

6.7) How to Screw and Glue Accurately..42

6.8) How to Sand Wood to Perfection..44

7) Make Sides AB...46

7.1) Mark-out XY Coords and Neck Pocket..47

7.2) Mark the Outside of Sides A..49

7.3) Mark-out the Interior of Sides A...51

7.4) Saw Out the Perimeter of Sides A...52

- 7.5) Saw Out the Insides of Sides A 52
- 7.6) If Needed, Thicken Sides A with Sides B 52
- 7.7) Ensure That the Neck Will Fit Perfectly 52
- 7.8) Rasp the Chamfer of Sides A 53

8) Make the Front Soundboard 54
- 8.1) Copy Sides AB Outline onto Front Soundboard 55
- 8.2) Mark-out the XY Coordinate Lines 55
- 8.3) Mark-out the Bridge Screw-Holes 57
- 8.4) Mark-out the Pickup Holes 57
- 8.5) Mark-out the Control Holes 57
- 8.6) Mark-out the Front Soundboard F-Holes 58
- 8.7) Sawing the Front Soundboard 59
- 8.8) Drilling the Front Soundboard 59
- 8.9) Cutting a Slot for the 5 Way Selector 60
- 8.10) Sanding the Front Soundboard Cut-outs 60

9) Make the Struts for the Soundboard 61
- 9.1) Mark Out the Struts 62
- 9.2) Cut Out the Struts 63

10) Glue the Struts Inside the Soundboard 64
- 10.1) Mark the Position of the Struts 65
- 10.2) Glue and Tape the Struts 65
- 10.3) Use Sandbags to Hold the Assembly Flat 65

10.4) Tune the struts..66

11) Glue the Sides AB onto the Front Soundboard..68

    11.1) Glue Together...69

    11.2) Shape Up...69

    11.3) Use as a Template to Mark All Other Layers...............................69

    11.4) Mark-out the XY Coordinate Lines on Every Layer...................69

12) Add Sides C and D to the Body...70

    12.1) Add Sides C, with glue and screws..72

    12.2) Add Sides D, with glue and screws...73

13) Make the Body Back Cover..75

    13.1) Mark-out Back Cover..77

    13.2) Cut-out Back Cover...77

    13.3) Drill Screw Holes...77

    13.4) Drill Countersinks...77

14) Make the Internal Bridge Mechanism..78

    14.1) Mark-out and Cut-out All Bridge Parts.......................................79

    14.2) Glue Together the Bridge Back Block..79

    14.3) Glue the Buttresses onto the Block..80

    14.4) Glue the Bridge Block onto the Struts..80

    14.5) Glue and Screw On the Bridge Tongue..80

15) Finishing the Wood Surfaces...81

    15.1) Guitars vs Furniture vs Buildings..81

15.2) Oil vs Lacquer vs Paint..81

15.3) Compatible Stains...82

15.4) Make a Handle for the Body..82

15.5) Final Grain Raising and Fine Sanding.......................................83

15.6) Simple Danish Oil Finish: Easiest...84

15.7) Using Spirit Based Stain: Optional...85

15.8) Sunburst Staining: Exotic..85

15.9) Bright Water-Based Dyes: Exotic...86

15.10) Water-based Lacquer: Recommended....................................87

15.11) Satin Finish..88

15.12) High Gloss Finish: Optional..89

15.13) Spray Painting...91

16) Fitting Pickups..93

17) Controls and Wiring..96

17.1) Soldering..97

17.2) Potentiometers..97

17.3) Tone Control and Capacitor..97

17.4) 5-Way Switch..98

17.5) The Earth Wiring..98

17.6) The Signal Wiring...99

17.7) Touch Testing the Wiring..99

17.8) Tap Testing Pickups and Controls..100

17.9) Optional Testing with a Multi-Meter..101

18) The Neck..102

18.1) Choosing a Compatible Neck...102

18.2) Make the Neck Shim..103

18.3) Dressing Frets..103

18.4) Finishing the Wood of the Neck..104

18.5) Fitting a Nut...104

18.6) Fitting Tuners...104

18.7) Adjusting the Neck Truss-rod..105

19) Final Assembly...108

19.1) Strap Buttons...108

19.2) Bridge...108

19.3) Screwing the Neck On...108

20) Final Set-up...109

20.1) Put the Strings On..109

20.2) Set the Neck Tightly..109

20.3) Bridge Height...109

20.4) Neck Pocket Shim...110

20.5) Bridge Intonation by Measurement...111

20.6) Bridge Intonation by Tuner..113

20.7) Bridge Intonation by Ear..113

20.8) Pickup Heights...114

20.9) Pickup Poles...114

20.10) Headstock Nut...114

20.11) String Trees..118

20.12) Happy Playing, and Maintenance...118

21) This Series of Guitars and Books...120

22) Acknowledgements..122

1.1) Quick and Easy to Make

The laminated birch plywood construction is easy to cut out and assemble, screw and glue. It requires only a few tools, and just a few wood-working skills, which can be learnt during the project. A good domestic DIY toolkit will have most of the tools needed. No professional routers nor drill stands are needed. You will need either a good hand coping-saw, or a faster motorised scroll-saw, to cut out each of five layers of the body construction. Any industry-standard S-type or T-type guitar neck is used, which simply screws onto the industry-standard neck pocket. You could buy all new parts and make a very glamorous guitar. You could, at tiny cost, find most parts from pre-used donor guitars, and get an equally great playing musical instrument.

1.2) Innovative Pat. Pend. Design

The internal bridge mechanism is a new invention for which Clive filed U.S. provisional patent application US 62/514,789. It is used on all the Rees semi-acoustic guitars. It does two things:

It balances and stabilises the forces on the guitar front, so that a thin responsive soundboard can be used, without risk of stress-warping

It restrains the modes of vibration of the bridge, such that sustain is long, and the playing feel is more like an electric guitar than an acoustic guitar. This makes the instrument easier to play well. It can have a very low adjustable action. The bridge is designed to resist the onset of feedback when playing loud electric.

The Rees semi-acoustic guitar is U.K. Registered Design number 6010985.

You are welcome to make and sell a few guitars of this design on condition that you declare that the original designer is Clive M. Rees of Cambridge England.

1.3) Industry Standard Neck Joint

In the middle of the guitar is the joint between the neck and the body. As on all Fender guitars, there is a standard size pocket in the body into which any standard neck fits. Four big screws from the back plate hold the neck firmly into the pocket. There is a small difference in the pocket end shape, but not position, between S-type necks, and T-type necks. Either can be made to work perfectly on any Rees guitar.

The origin of the coordinate system used throughout the technical drawings, is at the centre-line of the guitar, and at the body end of the neck pocket. This ensures that a wide variety of necks are going to fit the body. It makes it easy to independently verify the positions of parts on the body and parts on the neck, so that the intonation of the overall guitar is perfect.

1.4) Playing Acoustic

These Rees semi-acoustics, are not as loud as normal big body acoustic guitars. So they may not be as good as them for acoustic stage performance. They are considerably louder than most traditional semi-acoustic guitars, and have better bass response. So they are ideal for practice at home in the evening, without annoying your neighbours, or waking your child. The action can be very low, and either light or heavy electric strings can work well.

They are good for recording, if you have a quiet background environment. They have a nicely even frequency response from bass to treble.(Most traditional semi-acoustic guitars have feeble bass responses!)

1.5) Playing Electric

The electric voice character, as you might expect, is strongly determined by the pickups used. So we have several guitars in this family which each use different pickups. However, compared to a solid-body guitar, these Rees semi-acoustics have considerably more character, and wide dynamic feel to exploit. That makes them work extremely well, and even sound surprisingly nice, with tiny practice amps, and low cost pickups. Of course, they will sound even better with top quality pickups and performance amps.

The onset of feedback is a critical characteristic of any electric guitar. Rees semi-acoustics are designed to progressively feedback around the sound level of a full drum kit bashed fairly hard, without drum amplification. That means that with a small adjustment of positions of drums, amp, guitar, you can perform anywhere from small pub, to big venues with extra miked PA for all musicians. You will anywhere have full control of your guitar, from sweet clean, to chugging the dirt with screaming feed-back. You can even sensibly do the feedback stuff at home, or in a small pub, with a bit of energetic playing.

1.6) About the Author

Clive M. Rees has an M.A. degree in Engineering of The University of Cambridge, and an M.Sc. degree in Medical Electronics of The University of London. He is an inventor of patents, and was a successful manufacturing company technical director. He worked in electronics design, and software development, for 30 years. He designed new medical electronic instruments, and new computer graphics electronics and software. During that time he occasionally made guitars as a hobby. He has been a full-time self-employed Luthier, making professional guitars, for the past 12 years. He designed and made electric guitars; basses; and electronic effects pedals. You can see and hear these many different Rees instruments at www.rees-electric-guitars.com.

2) Various Guitar Construction Methods

Let us compare the construction of various traditional guitar types, and new guitar types. I assess the skills needed; build time required; and difficulty of making. I rate each guitar type for build difficulty, relative to the original Spanish Guitar set at 10:

2.1) Traditional Spanish Guitars – difficulty 10

The body front is made of flat thin softwood, such as spruce, in two halves. The back is made of thin hardwood in two halves that is steamed and bevelled slightly. The sides are made of thin hardwood that is heavily steamed and very gently bent extensively around templates. The joints between the sides and the front and back are complicated and require very many clamps during glueing up. There is much precision detail work to be done to add purflings on every outside edge.

2.2) Traditional Flat-top Steel String Guitars – difficulty 12

Construction is much like the Spanish guitar, but must be a lot stronger to support the higher tension of steel strings. The internal bracing of the soundboard is different and stronger. A steel truss rod in the neck prevents it from bending. (e.g. Martin)

2.3) Traditional F-Hole Arch-top Guitars – difficulty 20

These can be semi-acoustic, having a completely hollow body (e.g. Gibson ES175). They can alternatively be chambered, having a solid block between front and back, under the bridge.(e.g Gibson ES335) The chambered guitars have much better resistance to feedback. They are often loosely called semi-acoustic.

The back and sides are made something like the Spanish guitar, but with a different overall shape. The front soundboard is made in a very different and more complicated way, in order to have an arched shape. The front is made of multiple laminates of very thin maple, glued together. The arch shape is produced by squeezing the laminate between a shaped front and back template block. Effectively this is a way of making an arch shaped plywood front.

2.4) Traditional Solid Electric Guitars – difficulty 5

The body is made of two or three pieces of solid wood which must be accurately jointed, and glued together with clamps. Precision plane skills are needed to make these joints exactly flat and square. Then the pockets for the neck and pickups and controls are cut out using a power router. The router can be guided by computer on a NC rig. A hand router can be used with accurate templates to guide it. The templates must be made before a guitar can be made. It is possible to cut out the pockets for the neck and the pickups with a hand chisel, if you have good chiselling skills.

2.5) Rees Semi-Acoustic Guitars – difficulty 3

The body of a Rees Semi-Acoustic guitar is made by simply screwing and gluing together five laminates of birch plywood.

The only wood-cutting skill required is to use a hand coping saw, or a power scroll saw, to cut the curved shapes of each laminate, with some cut-outs. No specialist tools, nor jigs, nor clamps, are needed.

3) Construction of the Rees Semi-Acoustic

3.1) The Laminated Body

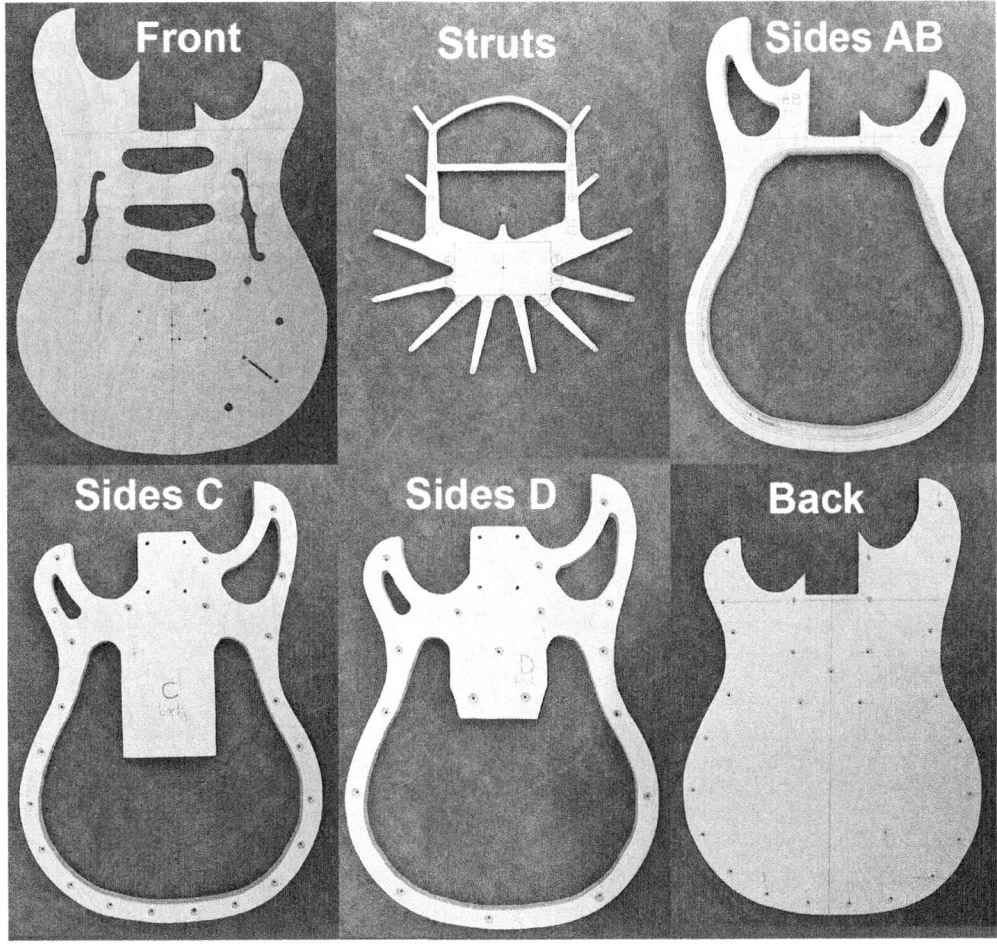

The body of the guitar is made from five pieces of birch plywood laminate. From front to back, these are:

Front Soundboard,
   with struts glued inside it;
glued to Sides AB;
glued to Sides C;
glued to Sides D;
with a screw-on screw-off Back Cover.

These five pieces are glued together to make a hollow body. The curved shapes of each laminate need to be cut out with a coping-saw, or a faster power scroll-saw. The accuracy of the thicknesses, and precision of the assembly, is pre-determined by using high quality plywood. You will not need the hard-learnt skill of planing wood flat, parallel, and square.

Here are two technical drawing of the centre cross-section of the complete guitar body. The first has dimensions and plywood thicknesses in inches. The second is in metric units.

Please note well that the pickups are fixed onto the back centre spine of laminate C. This dwg shows P90 pickups for simple clarity. The same is true for all pickup types on Rees semi-acoustics. The front soundboard does not touch the pickups at all, and is free to vibrate the sound of the guitar without being bogged down by heavy pickups. (most traditional semi-acoustic guitars have the pickups mounted on the front which deadens the acoustic tone).

3.2) Typical Body Centre Cross-Section in Inches

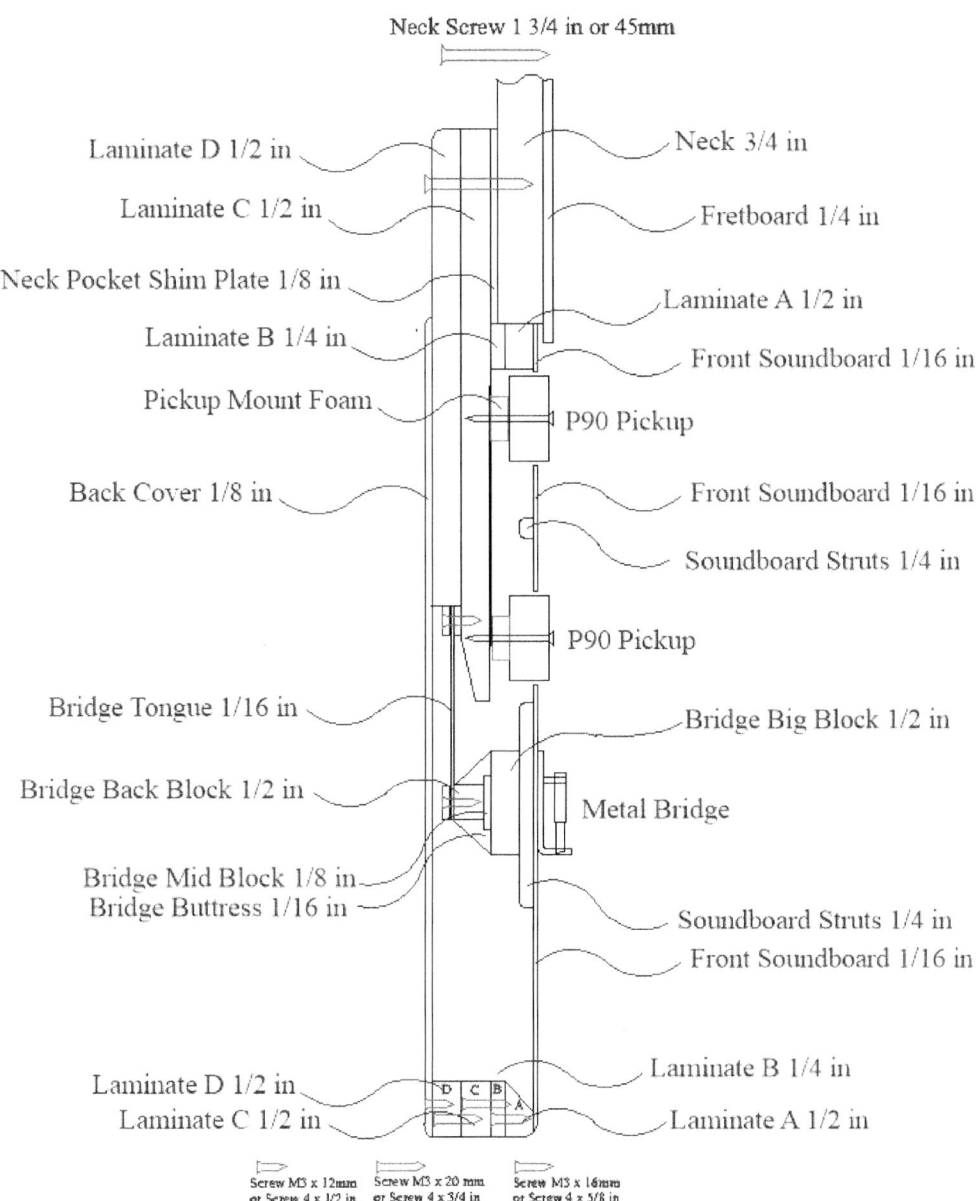

3.3) Typical Body Centre Cross-Section in Metric

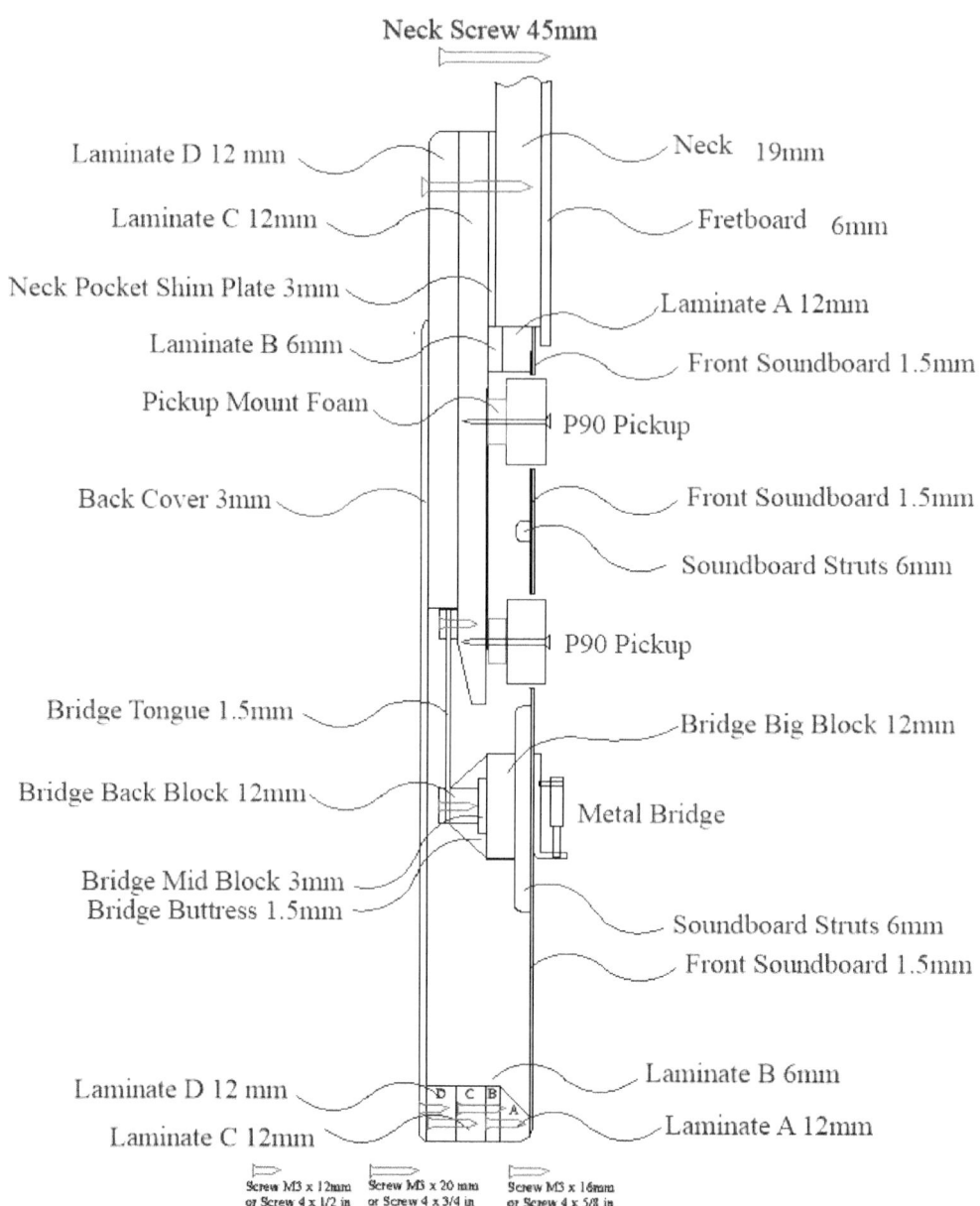

3.4) The Soundboard with Struts

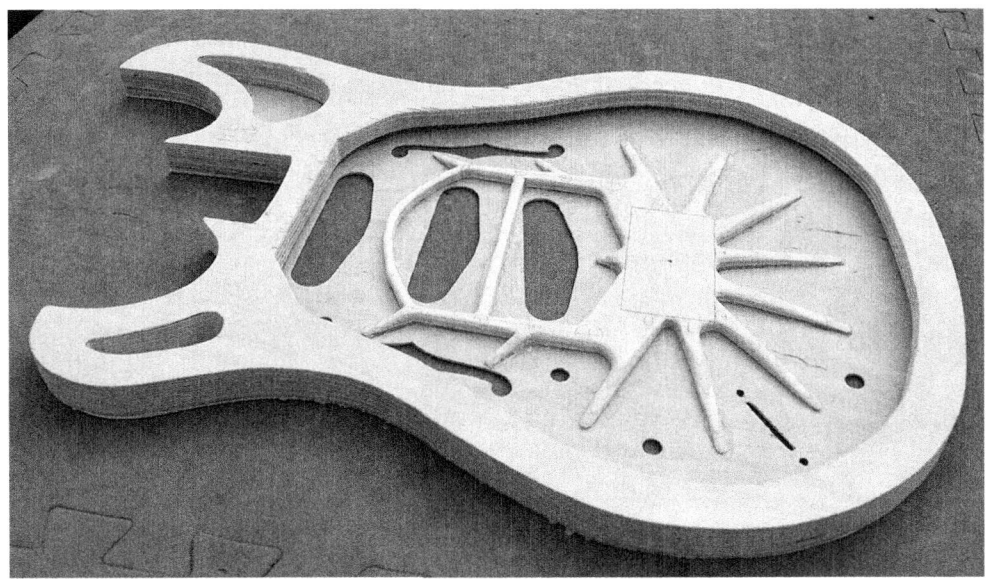

All guitar soundboards connect the small but strong vibrations of the strings, through the bridge, to a much larger volume of air. To be loud, the soundboard needs to be large enough, and have good depth of vibration. Treble frequencies want stiffness in the wood to sound crisp. Bass frequencies want flexibility in the wood to move a larger volume of air. The soundboard needs a low resonant frequency to amplify the strings right down to the bottom string. A thick soundboard, say 1/8 inch or 3mm, would be too stiff, with very poor bass rendition. That is why traditional plywood guitars have such a poor reputation. The thinnest plywood until recently was 1/8 inch. However, with the invention of 1.5mm = 1/16in birch plywood, we are "3 leagues up the ball-game!"

The ideal way to cover all frequencies with fidelity is to design a soundboard that has variable stiffness from stiff in the middle to flexible at the outside. This principle is used in all good loudspeaker cones.

It is also used in the construction of traditional guitars, but has always been compromised by the need for the struts to be strong. The traditional struts must also hold back the strong twisting force of the strings on the bridge, which causes the soundboard to dive. This is the demise of many an old acoustic guitar.

On a Rees semi-acoustic guitar, the inside bridge mechanism balances the forces of the strings, so that the front soundboard is not twisted and dived. Having solved that problem, the design of the soundboard is essentially to be an uncompromised, made-of wood, loudspeaker cone! The ideal behaviour is stiff for high frequencies at the centre, and flexible for bass response at the perimeter. A smooth transition from centre to perimeter eliminates undesirable rattly resonances.

3.5) The Pat. Pend. Inside of the Bridge

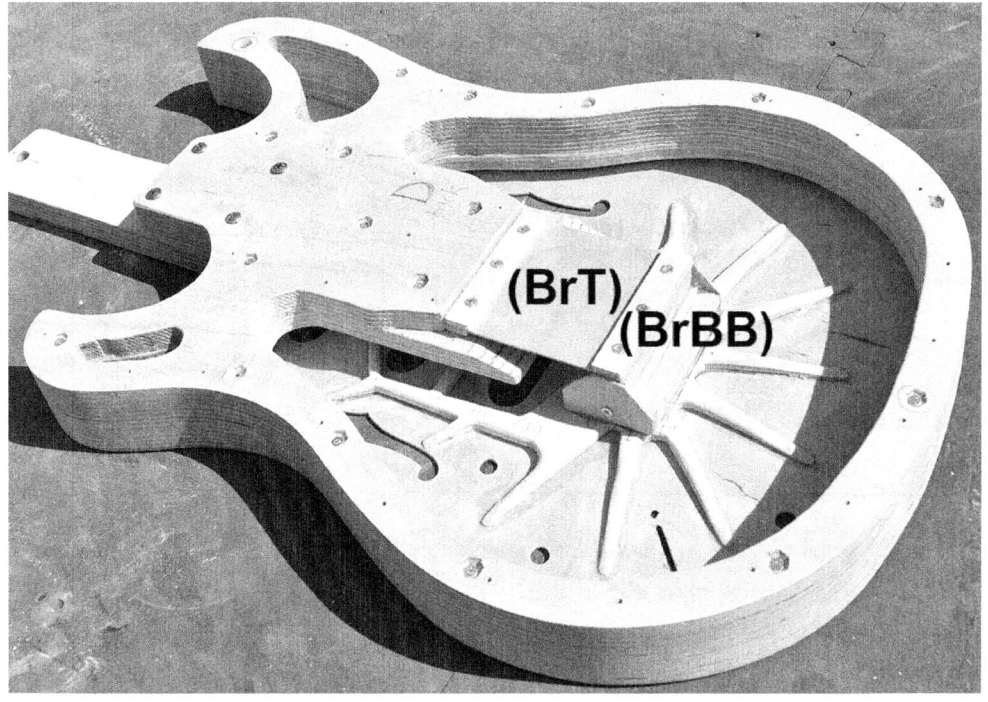

Here is a photo of the inside bridge mechanism. At the back of the front metal guitar bridge, is a sophisticated multi-laminate bridge back block **(BrBB)** of plywood. This is designed to be strong, rigid, and fairly light. In the middle of the photo is the 1/16 in =1.5mm thick bridge tongue **(BrT)** which connects the bridge back block to the central back spine of the guitar. The overall bridge back mechanism does two important jobs:

The tongue is in tension, and balances the tension of the strings on the front, so that the soundboard is no longer twisted to dive. It stabilises the whole guitar body, and reduces any soundboard warping with age, which would deteriorate the playing action of the guitar.

The tongue and the soundboard together, constrain the bridge to vibrate front to back as on an electric guitar; and not as a twisting vibration that acoustic guitar have. Sustain is enhanced, acoustic and electric. Electric feedback is controlled because the modes of vibration are constrained.

4) Parts and Materials

It is worth your while to find and buy all parts and materials, before you start this project. That way you can check, and double-check, that everything will fit together exactly. Check compatibility, and accuracy, as you progress through the three stages: from marking out wood; to cutting out wood; to finally glueing together wood parts.

It is worth reading this book from start to end, before getting into the buying and building details of your project. You will then avoid mistakes, and create a better guitar, to own and play.

4.1) Materials to Make This Guitar

Birch Plywoods in Inches

The direction of grain must be along the longer dimension
    Body Front Soundboard: 1/16in thick: 19in long x 16 in wide
    Soundboard Struts: 1/4in thick: 12in long x 12 in wide
    Laminate AB: 3/4in thick: 19in long x 16 in wide
      (or 3/8in+3/8in or 1/2in+1/4in)
    Laminate C: 1/2in thick: 19in long x 16 in wide
    Laminate D: 1/2in thick: 19in long x 16 in wide
    Body Back: 1/8in thick: 19in long x 16 in wide

A standard plywood sheet is 96in long in direction of grain, and 48in wide.
A sheet can be cut into 15 laminates:
5 off length of 19in (5x19in=95in)
3 off width of 16in (3x16in=48in)

Birch Plywoods in Metric

The direction of grain must be along the longer dimension
  Body Front Soundboard: 1.5mm thick: 485mm long x 400mm wide
  Soundboard Struts: 6mm thick: 300mm long x 300mm wide
  Laminate AB: 18mm thick: 485mm long x 400mm wide
    (or 9mm+9mm or 12mm+6mm)
    Laminate C: 12mm thick: 485mm long x 400mm wide

Laminate D: 12mm thick: 485mm long x 400mm wide mm

Body Back: 3mm thick: 485mm long x 400mm wide

A standard plywood sheet is 2440mm long in direction of grain, and 1220mm wide.

A sheet can be cut into 15 laminates:

5 off length of 485mm (5x485mm=2425mm)

3 off width of 400mm (3x400mm=1200mm)

Adhesives:

Evostick Resin W wood glue, or Titebond white wood glue

10 minute Epoxy 2-part glue

Temporary masking tape

Screws

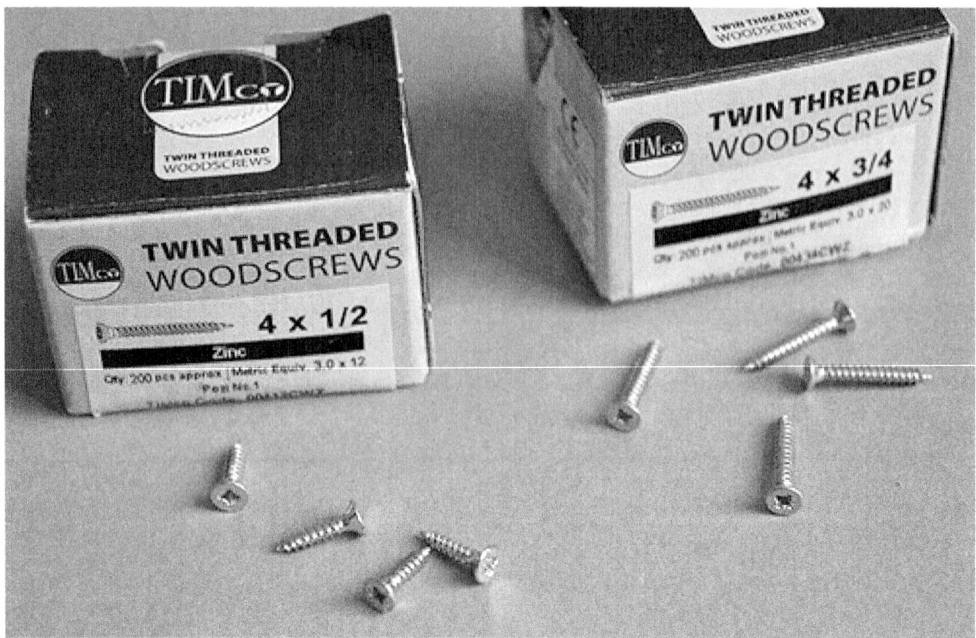

Using exactly the right screw sizes is very important. They must have countersunk heads. Twin-threaded are fastest to screw in and screw out. They have nice reliable constant thickness along the whole length of the shaft. Zinc plated look very good. Chrome plated or stainless steel are lovely and expensive if you can find them. Phillips screwdriver X slots look best. My favourites are made by TIMco.

> Box of No4 x 1/2in = M3mm x 12mm for back panel
> Box of No4 x 3/4in = M3mm x 18mm for middle laminates
> Optional: Box of No4 x 5/8in = M3mm x 15mm only if joining laminates A and B

Wood Finishing

> Water-based lacquer, or water-based varnish

optional spirit-based stain

optional surgical spirit to dilute and smoothly rub-in stain

Hum-Rejection

Optional sticky-back copper sheet

Wires

Insulated copper wires
 (optional various colours, solid or 7strand or 14 strand)

optional Tinned bare copper wire 22swg or similar

optional Coax wire

4.2) Parts to Make This Guitar:

Body Parts

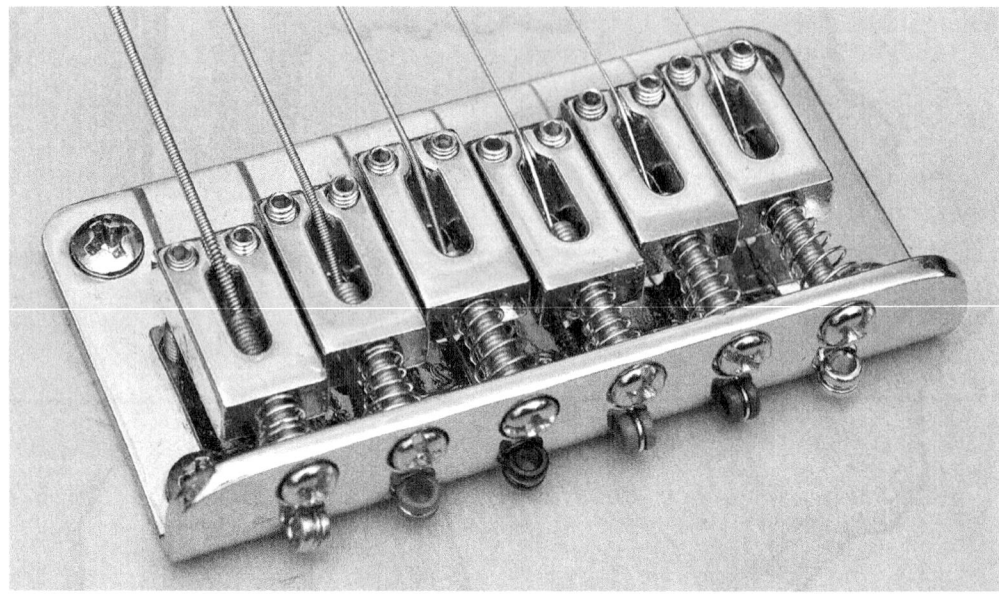

    S-Type Top-loader bridge
    5 off Bridge mounting screws
    2 off Strap buttons with screws and pads (big ones are safest)

Neck Parts

S-Type industry standard guitar neck with:
    Nut
    String tree or trees
    6-In-Line Tuners
    Neck Plate + 4off 45mm or 1 ¾ in neck screws

Pickups

    3 off S-Type single-coil pickups
    3 off plastic pickup covers (any colour)
    6 off bass pickup mounting screws
    Foam pads to support pickups

Electric Controls

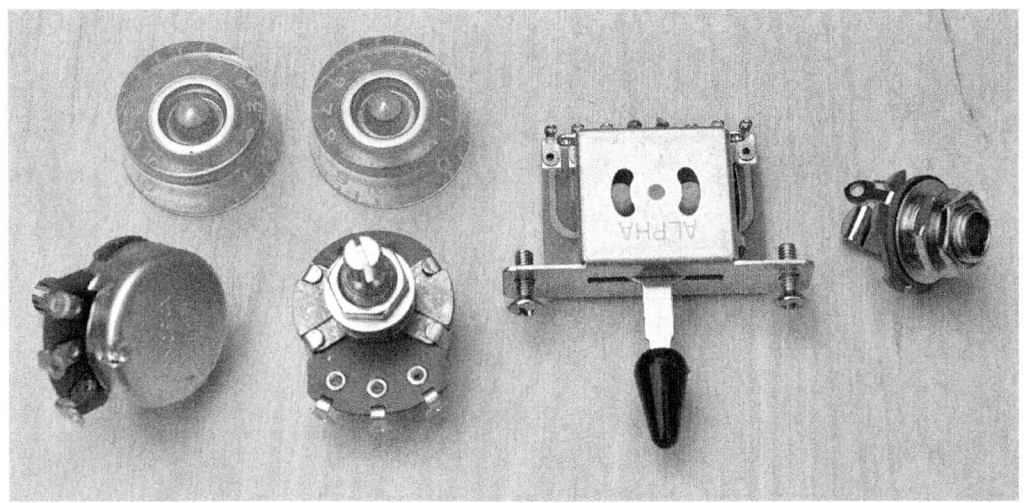

Any Lightweight Control Knobs: Volume and Tone

Potentiometers: Volume 250kA and Tone: 250kA

Tone capacitor: 33nF

5-way pickup selector switch + tip

¼ in Jack Socket

5) Tools

5.1) Drilling Tools

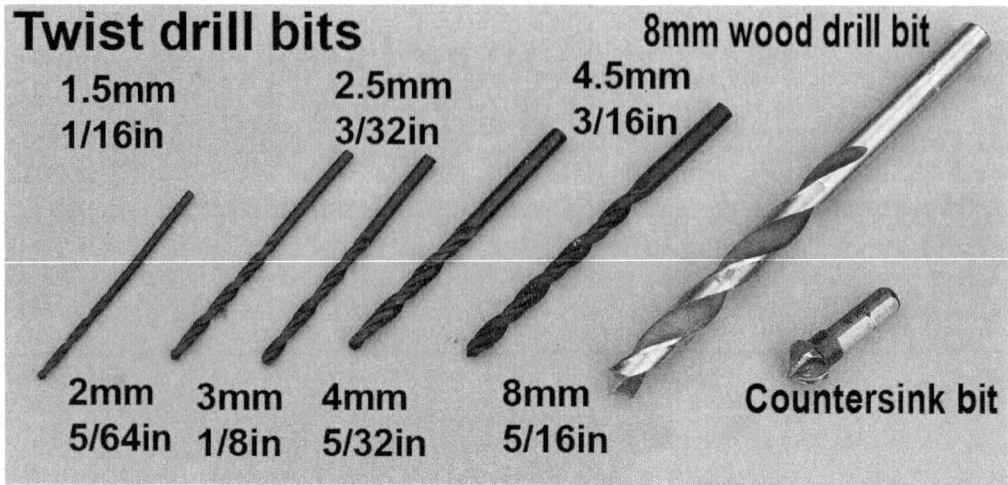

Small or medium size power drill

It does not need to be very powerful, and hand-held is fine if you are careful.

Having a stand for it is nice for accuracy, but not at all essential.

You must have all of the exact drill sizes:

Twist drill bits: 1.5mm; 2mm; 2.5mm; 3mm; 4mm; 4.5mm or
   1/16in; 5/64in; 3/32in; 1/8in; 5/32in; 3/16in.

Wood drill bit: 8mm or 5/16in

Countersink drill bit

5.2) Hand Coping Saw

Coping Saw with four 15tpi blades

The levers, at the top and bottom of the coping saw blade, allow the blade to be set in a choice of 8 different directions. We will use straight-on, and 90deg to left or right, blade directions.

5.3) Optional Powered Scroll Saw

A faster, more expensive, alternative to the coping saw, is a powered scroll saw. This is a photo of a scroll saw that is unplugged from electricity, and has the important safety guard removed for clarity of photo.

My recommendation is choose the most suitable scroll saw for you of:
- Hire a nice power scroll saw
- Buy a low cost power scroll saw
- Buy a pre-owned power scroll saw on Ebay

I like to use 15 tpi scroll-saw blades (15 teeth per inch).
You might prefer others. A wide variety are available.
Bigger teeth (less tpi) cut wood faster with rougher edges.
Smaller teeth (more tpi) cut wood slower; are easier to go round small corners;
Small teeth blades may be more difficult to keep on line on gentle long curves and straights.

5.4) Other Essential Tools

Marking Out

- Propelling pencil 0.5mm, HB leads
- Rubber
- Ruler
- Set-square
- Compass or circles template

Screw Fixing

- Phillips PH0 screwdriver
- Phillips PH1 screwdriver
- Phillips PH2 screwdriver
- Small flat blade screwdriver

Laminate Clamping

- 25 off 2 inch or 52mm bulldog clips
- 5lbs or 2 or 3kg of sand
- Polythene freezer bags

Wood Shaping

- Very sharp knife: pen-knife or scalpel
- Wood Rasp, flat and rounded, for overall smooth shaping

Wood Finishing

Wood Sandpapers:
3 or 4 sheets P80 grit; 2 sheets P120; 1 sheet P180; 1 sheet P240 grit

Lacquer Finishing

Lacquer polishing to satin finish:
Abralon pads (best) P400; P600; P1000; P2000 (1 or 2 pads each)
or Emery (wet and dry) papers: P400; P600; P1000; P1500 grit

Further optional lacquer polishing to gloss finish in addition:
1 pad Abralon P4000 (best), or Wire wool 0000 grade
Fareclar G3 regular polishing paste or equivalents
Fareclar G12 finishing polishing paste or equivalents

Electrics

Crocodile-nose pliers
Wire cutters
Soldering Iron, and solder wire:
   Budget priced iron, with traditional low-temperature lead solder, and safety care, or
   Temperature controlled iron of high-power, with modern high-temperature tin solder.

"Workbench"

Any flat surface larger than a guitar body,
   e.g. 18mm plywood or 18mm MDF
Thick polythene sheet, larger than a guitar body to prevent glue sticking to the "workbench"
Soft sheet of cloth or carpet or foam to prevent scratches on the body

5.4) Optional Useful Tools

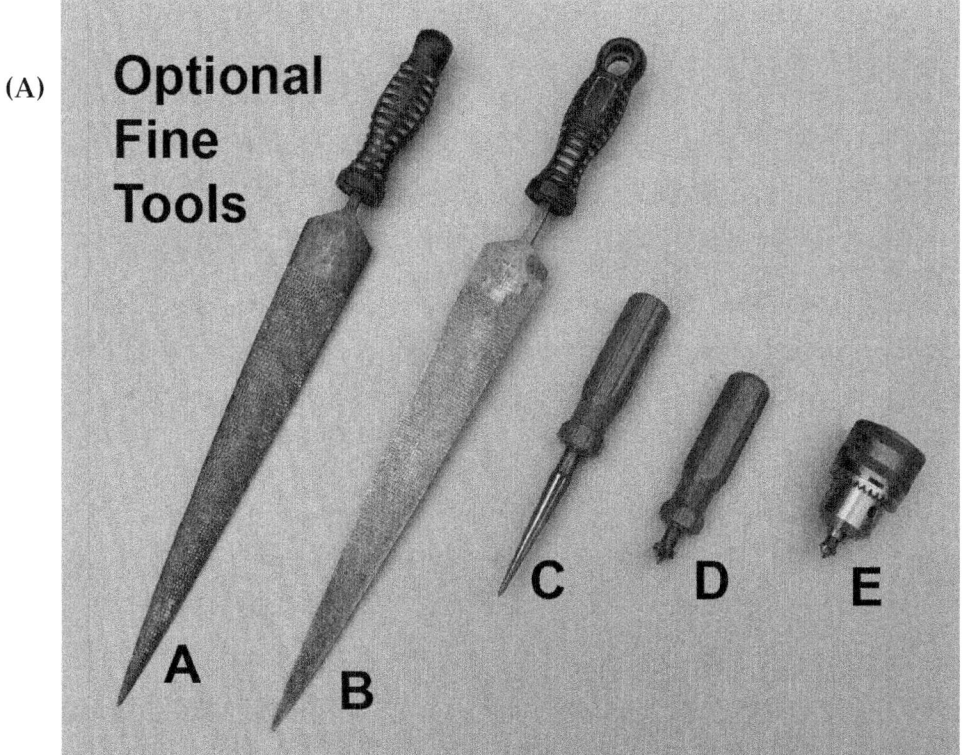

(A) Rough Dragon-tooth Rasp for overall shaping.

(B) Fine Dragon-tooth Rasp for smoothing shapes, between sawing and sanding.

(C) Reamer to cleanly enlarge drill holes with no splintering.

(D) Hand Countersink to perfect countersink screw holes after lacquering.

(E) Improvised Hand Countersink using a drill chuck

Sharp Chisel
Box Spanners
Long steel rule
wire cutter and stripper

Guitar string winder and cutter
Guitar Tuner

6) How to Use Your Tools with Best Skill

6.1) How to Mark Out Wood

Birch plywood has very fine grain. A 0.5mm propelling pencil with HB lead draws very accurate lines on it. Press just hard enough to draw clearly visible lines. Do not press too hard else the lines will dent the wood and require undesirable sanding to later remove.

Many of the dimensions are measured in the same XY coordinate system. The origin X 0 is at the centre of the guitar lengthways. The origin Y 0 is across the guitar at the body end of the neck pocket. Draw the centre line X 0 on every part with a ruler. Draw the Y 0 line at 90 deg to it with a set square.

Mark out laminate A and cut it out. You can then use it as a copy template to mark out all the other laminates' perimeters and insides. This greatly reduces the number of measurements to be marked around the curves.

6.2) How to Drill Holes Accurately

It is important to use fairly new undamaged high quality twist drills. Look closely at the cutting end of the drill bit to see that it is sharply ground, and perfectly symmetric on both sides. If it is not symmetric, or is damaged in detail at the cutting edge, it will slew to one side when drilling.

Hold or clamp the part to be drilled onto a horizontal surface. Take great care to hold your power-drill so that the drill bit is vertical, both front-to-back, and side-to-side.

When drilling a hole completely through the wood, go gently as the drill gets near to exiting the wood. Hold the wood firmly on a flat piece of ½ in plywood scrap, to prevent splintering on the edges of the hole exit.

For small holes, twist drills are fine. For medium size holes, first drill the hole at 2mm or 5/64 in for precision. Then re-drill it to the final size. For large holes, use a wood drill which has a centre point to guide it's position.

6.3) Sawing All the Curves

There is a lot of curved shape sawing to be done in this project, due to the multi laminate construction. The good news is that these curved shapes are not themselves critical to the final performance of the guitar. The fact that birch plywood is manufactured exactly flat, with very accurate thickness is a huge benefit. It eliminates most of the accuracy, and squaring, and alignment problems of traditional solid-wood carpentry. Solid wood guitar construction requires advanced skill by the carpenter; or precision templates with hand-held routers; or a computer controlled CAD-CAM system. The biggest decision in our tool choice is: hand sawing with a coping saw; or powered sawing with a scroll saw.

6.4) How to Use a Coping Saw

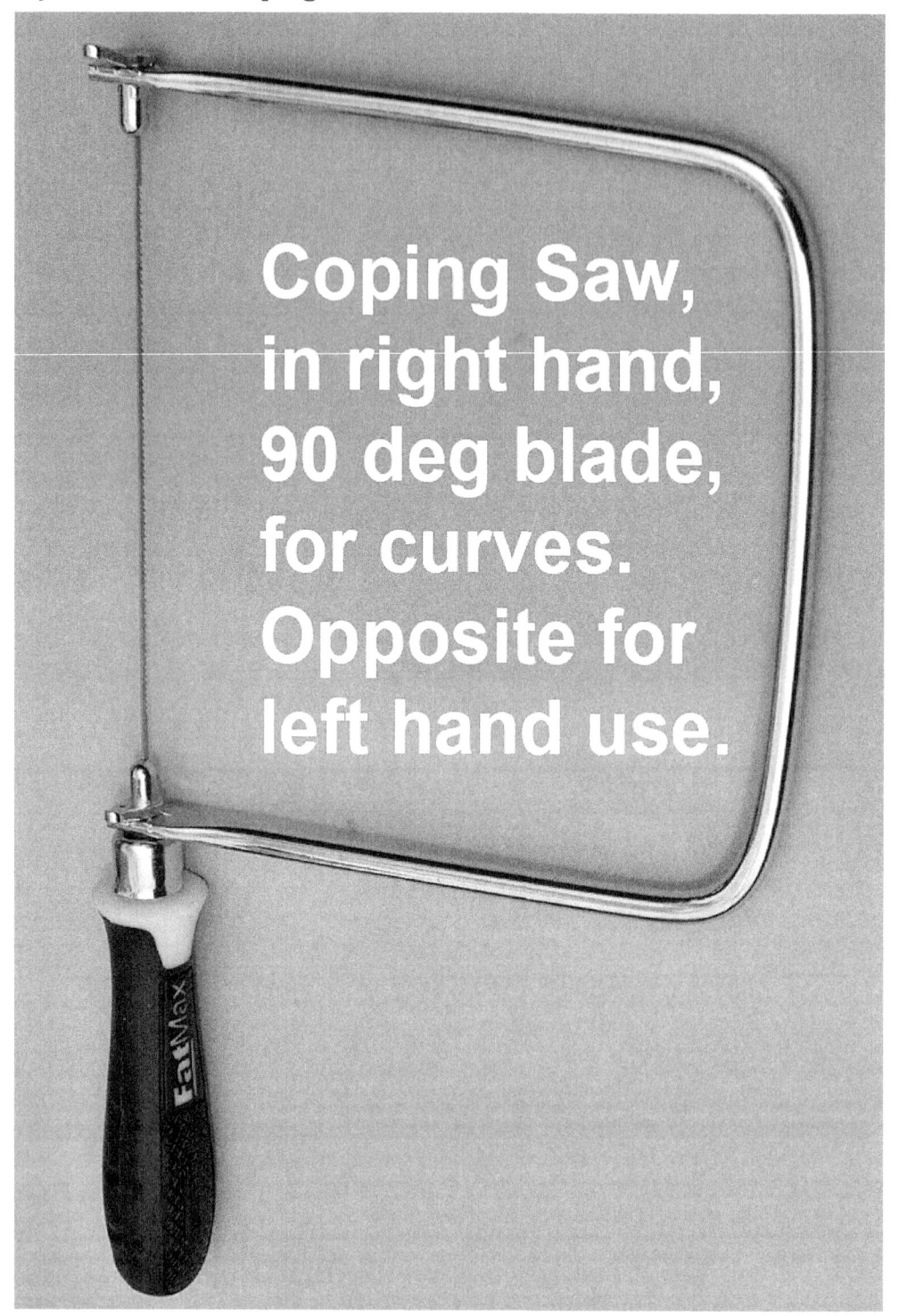

Coping Saw, in right hand, 90 deg blade, for curves. Opposite for left hand use.

The photo above shows a coping saw with the saw blade at 90deg direction for right-hand use around big curves. Left-handed guitar makers can set the blade the other way around, and cut the guitar curves around the other way. The earlier photo in the 5.2) Tools chapter, shows a coping saw with the blade straight in-line. Observe the difference of direction of the two blade rotation levers, one at the top, and one at the bottom, of the saw blade. Screwing the handle, in or out, relative to the rest of the saw frame, enables your to tighten or loosen the blade, and finally tighten it, in the desired blade rotation, before proceeding with cutting. Coping saw blades have a small pin at each end of the blade, which hooks into each of the two rotating anchor pieces.

You must hold flat, and firmly, the plywood laminate being sawed. You can hold the plywood with your other non-sawing hand. You might, most reliably, clamp it, and several times re-clamp it, to the edge a garden table.

Hold the coping saw so that the blade is exactly vertical, so that all cutting is square to the laminate surface. The handle is below, and the blade teeth point down, so that the cutting stroke is down. Practice on scrap wood, before you carve out a guitar.

Coping sawing does not create huge amounts of sawdust. You could do this indoors, with plenty of window ventilation. However, please take care. If you live with a partner, or a family, or friends, consult them first. Completely clean up afterwards, in detail.

For each plywood laminate, firstly, cut out the perimeter of the guitar. You can do this entirely with the saw blade at 90deg to the saw frame. Hold the coping saw in your right hand. With your left hand, hold down, and control, the laminate of plywood. Position the plywood laminate over the front right edge of your garden table, with your left hand. Throughout the cutting of the whole perimeter, the frame of the scroll saw hangs out to the right.

If you are left-handed, do the right-left mirror opposite of all this.

For inside cut-outs of shapes, first drill a hole in the laminate, in the inside shape, with your 8mm = 5/16in wood drill. Undo the saw blade at it's top; push it through the new hole; attach it to the saw with working tension.

The large inside body hollow is most easily cut with the saw blade at 90deg to it's frame. You can finish the middle parts of the body hollow by re-setting the coping saw blade direction at straight-on. If you get into a tight spot, where the saw frame is tangled and inhibiting rotation, go back, and then cut out another small area of unwanted material. That space will win you more room to manoeuvre for the next cut.

Change the blade for a new one as soon as it gets blunted. You first feel that when it gets more difficult to control accurately on curves, and to go around sharp corners. You might need 4 to 6 blades for the project.

6.5) How to Use a Power Scroll Saw

Safety First

Please beware that power scroll saws can very quickly cut off wrongly-placed fingers, if you are stupidly careless. Please use the compatible safety guards supplied by the scroll saw manufacturer, and follow their safety advice.

Any Scroll Saw

My Proxxon scroll saw is my favourite Luthier's tool. Like a fine sports car, it has big power, and rushes around corners with great enthusiasm. Also, like most fine sports cars, it is a bit expensive! I chose it for it's ability to cut through 2 inch = 50mm hardwoods. Most scroll saws do not have the strength to do that. However, birch plywood up to 18mm thickness, is easy to cut nicely with the most inexpensive amateur scroll saws. I also have an old Draper scroll saw which I bought new, 15 years ago, for about £120, and it was used in making my first 80 guitars. It is getting a bit wheezy now, but still works perfectly well for cutting 18mm birch plywood.

Accuracy

Check that the saw table is horizontal, and that the saw blade is vertical, with the teeth pointing down. Use safety guards. See the scroll saw user manual. Practice outside curves, and a variety of inside curves, on scrap wood, before you carve out a guitar.

Change the blade for a new one as soon as it gets blunted. You first feel that when it gets harder to control accurately on curves, and to go around sharp corners. You might need 3 to 5 blades for the project. 15 tpi are my favourite blades.

For inside cut-outs of shapes, first drill a hole in the laminate, in the inside of the shape, with your 8mm = 5/16in wood drill. Undo the saw blade at it's top, push it through the new hole, attach it to the saw with working tension.

6.6) How to Shape Wood

Rasping

After glueing the laminates together, you will have very rough sides on the guitar. You will need to remove quite a lot of wood to get smooth square sides. Use a rasp of the best quality you can afford. Choose one that is flat on one side, and rounded on the other. Use the flat side of the rasp for outside curves, and use the rounded side for inside curves. It will get used a lot.

Take care to hold the rasp square to the wood, so that you end up with all sides of the guitar being square to the front and back. Do some work with the guitar on it's back and some work with the guitar on it's front. Be gentle when going near sharp corners. Frequently view carefully, in detail, the shape you are creating. You might check the edges with a carpenter's L square.

Do not use a rasp on the front soundboard or the back. It creates too many splinters on thin plywood. Use rough sanding for the body front and back.

Rough Sanding Straight and Square

Use P80 grit sandpaper of best quality. Wrap the sandpaper around a flat rectangular hard rubber sanding block, or a 4 ½ inch by 3 inch by ½ inch plywood block. Take care to hold the block square against the edges you are sanding. Do some work with the guitar on it's back and some work with the guitar on it's front. Be gentle when going near sharp corners. Frequently view carefully, in detail, the shape you are creating. You might check the edges with a carpenter's L square.

Rough Sanding Outside Curves

Do as above with the sanding block. Add curved motions to your hand movement.

Rough Sanding Inside Curves

You can not use a sanding block, but you still want the sides of the guitar to be square to the front and back. Wrap your sandpaper around a cylinder like a drink can.

6.7) How to Screw and Glue Accurately

Carpenters most often clamp wood together after applying glue to both surfaces. They clamp very lightly, then slide the wood into exact position, then tighten up the clamps. A problem with using this method for guitars, is that you need 20 or more clamps. Another disadvantage, is that you can not do any further work on it while the glue is drying, probably overnight. However, screwing and glueing works extremely well, and is easier to do.

Firstly screw together the parts accurately without any glue. Then undo the parts and apply glue to both surfaces. Then finally screw the parts together. You can continue to do more work on this assembly, as it is structurally rigid before the glue has set.

In detail, for any "top" part screwed onto any "bottom" part: Drill 3mm or 1/8in all the screw holes in the top part. Countersink drill them all. Check that the screws fit nicely, and are recessed slightly below the surface of the top part. Align the top part on the bottom part accurately. Drill 2mm or 5/64in, for the full length of the screw, through the centres of two opposite screw holes. Twist screws into these two holes. Check that the parts are perfectly aligned. If not, undo one or both screws, choose one or both new holes, drill and try screwing again. When you have two parts aligned nicely with two screws, drill all the holes and twist in all screws.

Undo all screws. Apply white glue to both surfaces. The amount of squirted glue is shown in this photo, then flatten it to wet and cover all the two wood surfaces evenly. I find cut-up old credit cards to be good glue spreaders. Work fairly quickly, so the glue does not start drying too soon.

Make sure both surfaces are completely wet everywhere with glue. It is better to use too much than too little. Too much glue results in a lot squirting out the sides, when the parts are screwed together. It is easily wiped off, with kitchen roll paper, or a wet rag. Too little glue results in a weak or rattly dry joint, into which it is extremely difficult to insert glue later.

6.8) How to Sand Wood to Perfection

Sanding (or polishing) Under the Microscope

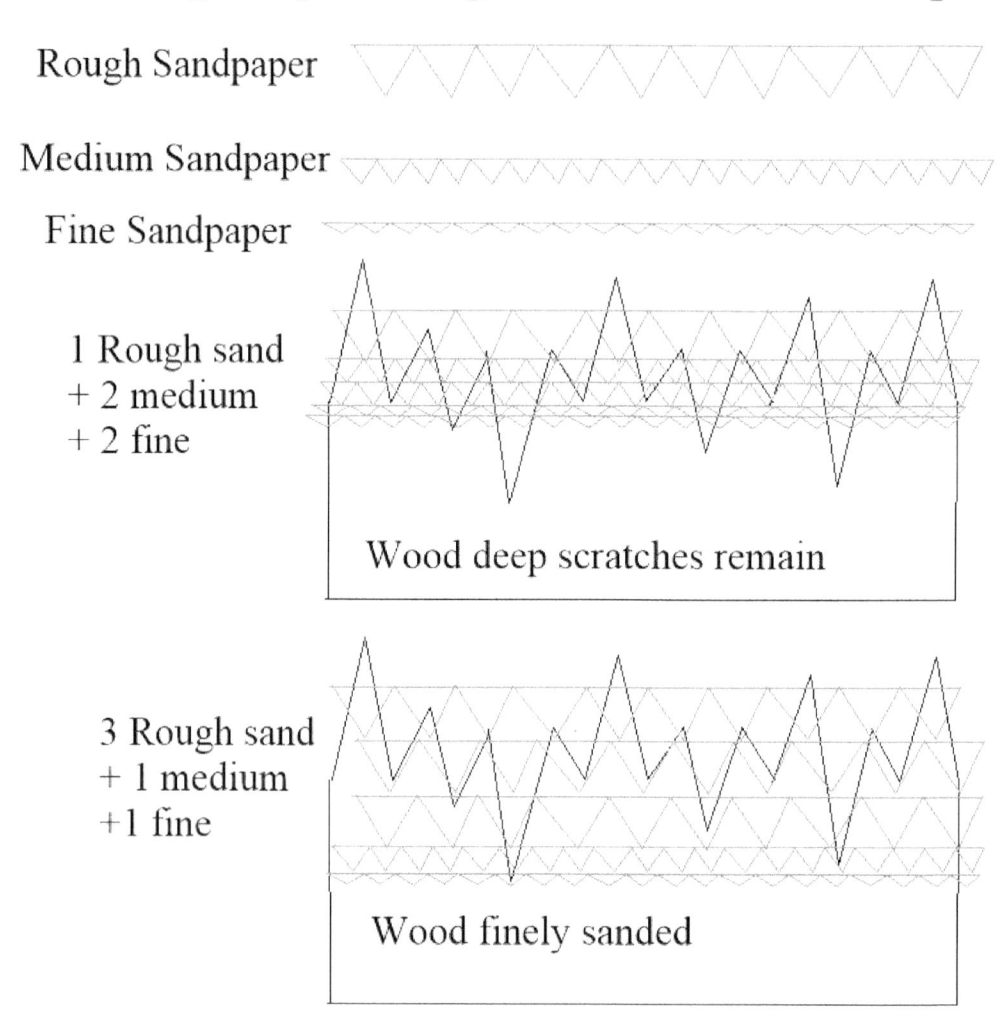

Rough Sandpaper

Medium Sandpaper

Fine Sandpaper

1 Rough sand
+ 2 medium
+ 2 fine

Wood deep scratches remain

3 Rough sand
+ 1 medium
+1 fine

Wood finely sanded

Rough wood has hills and valleys of a wide variety of random shapes and depths. Several stages of sanding are needed to transform this to a perfectly flat plain, free of any unsightly deeper scratches. The tops of the hills are very easily removed by rubbing with any sandpaper. The valleys and deepest scratches are much harder to remove! In order to remove all scratches at the bottom of all valleys, you need to remove wood evenly over the entire surface, and down in depth to the bottom of the scratches in the deepest valleys!

It is vitally important, while sanding, to not pick up any bigger bit of grit on the sandpaper. That big grit particle would then carve deeper scratches to ruin your work-so-far. Keep your sandpaper clean and unclogged, by brushing it or washing it, at every stage.

Hunting down any embarrassing scratches, requires a particular lighting scene: The light comes from just one source in the distance: indoors from one window; or indoors from one light bulb; or outdoors from the sun. These are the best lights to detect all possible scratches. View the surfaces of the guitar closely, against the light.

Outdoors Sunlight:
Excellent viewing, hold your guitar towards the sun. Look at the guitar. Do not look at the sun. Directly viewing the sun will probably damage your eyesight.

Outdoors cloud-light:
Useless, do not use. The light comes from all directions, and muddles and hides your view of scratches.

Indoors daytime cloud-light:
In order to direct light from a single source, have just one window in the room clear to the sky, and other window curtains closed.

Indoors evening or night light:
Have just one light-bulb or spot-light lit onto the guitar which you view from the other side.

Look, look, and look again, at your work for scratches. It will be impossible to remove them after staining and lacquer.

The drawings above shows you why there are 3 golden rules for sanding:
1) Spend a huge amount of time doing rough sanding, until that is done to perfection, with zero deeper scratches. Skimping on rough sanding is sure to result in disaster. Doing it right, can be followed by fairly easy medium sanding, and very easy fine sanding.
2) Look in great detail at your work, frequently, at every stage, with optimum scratch-detection lighting.
3) Keep your sandpaper clean at all stages.

7) Make Sides AB

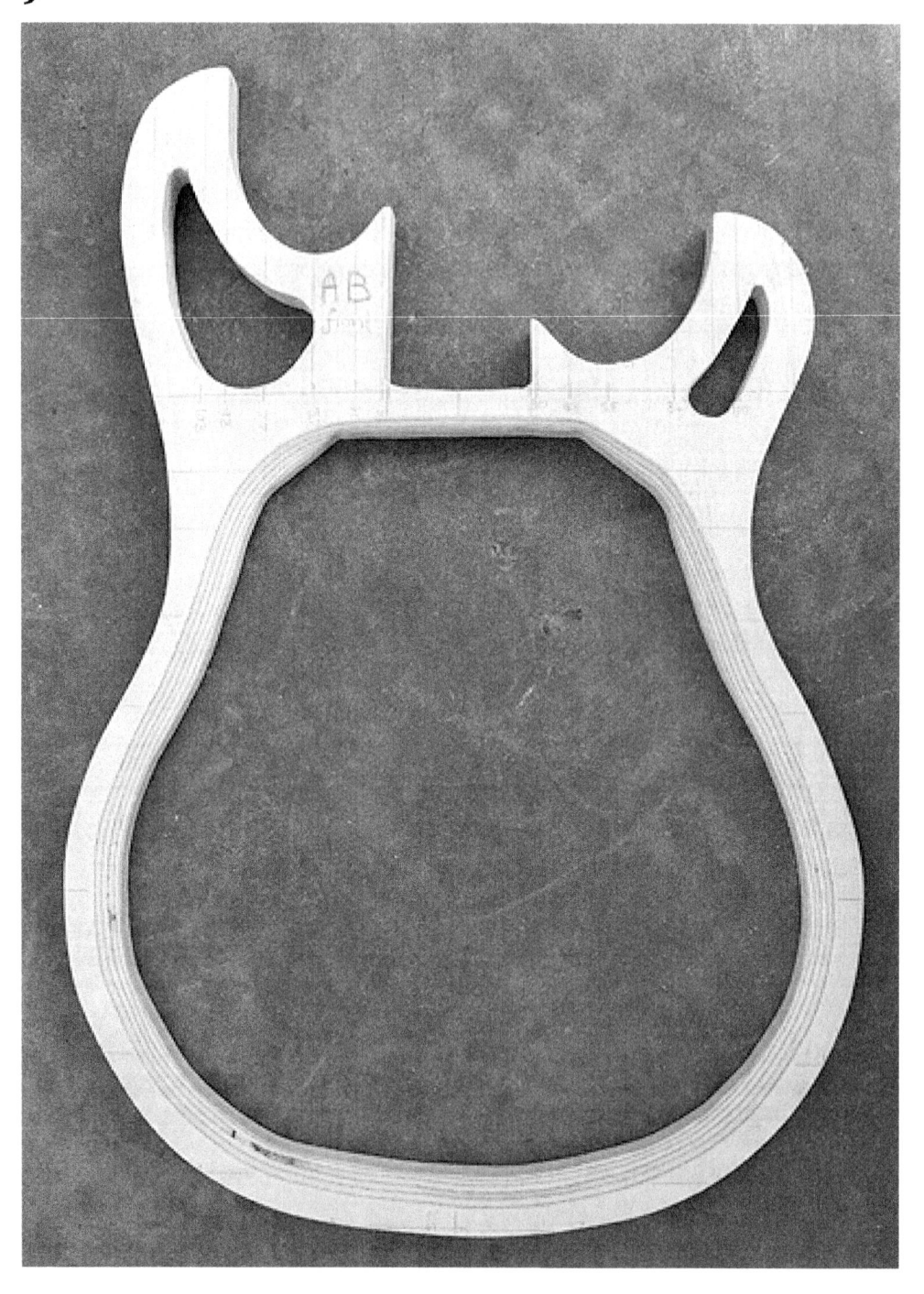

7.1) Mark-out XY Coords and Neck Pocket

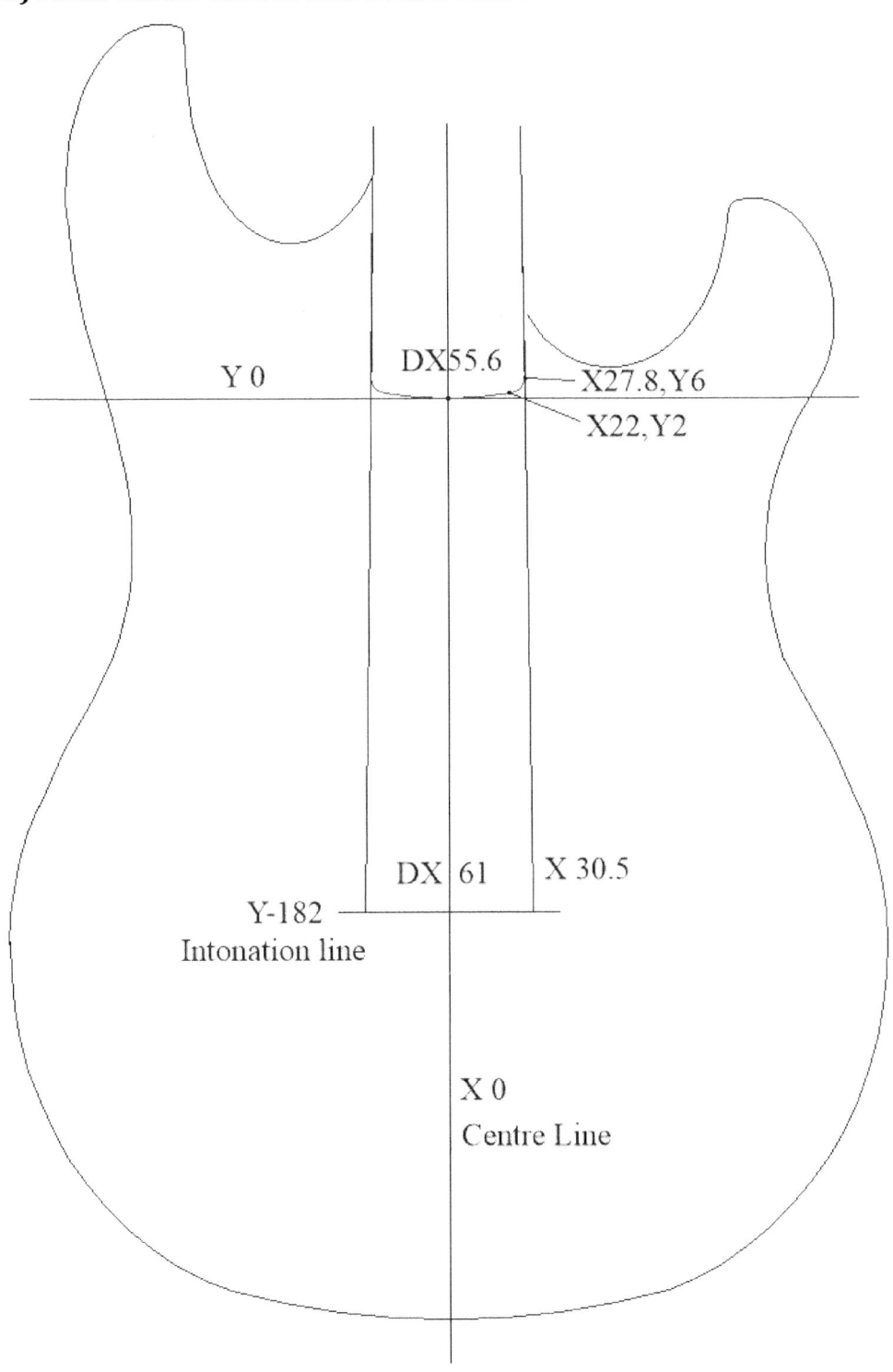

Y 0

DX 55.6

X27.8, Y6

X22, Y2

DX 61

X 30.5

Y-182
Intonation line

X 0
Centre Line

The origin lines of the coordinate system, X0 and Y0 should be marked on every laminate. They provide the accuracy and alignment of all parts.

The neck and the neck pocket are not exactly square. They are slightly wider at the bridge end, and slightly narrower at the headstock end. The slight angle of each side is very critical, so that the guitar strings, neck, pickups, and bridge all line up together along the centre of the guitar.

Take great care in all marking-out. It is not just a rough guide. The accuracy of the final build is totally dependent upon the accuracy of the marking-out!

The neck pocket is draw above for a strat compatible neck, which has a slightly curved end to it at Y0. A neck pocket for a tele compatible neck would have a straight square end to the pocket at the same Y0. Both have rounded corners. Check that the end of your guitar neck looks the same as the neck pocket mark-out.

7.2) Mark the Outside of Sides A

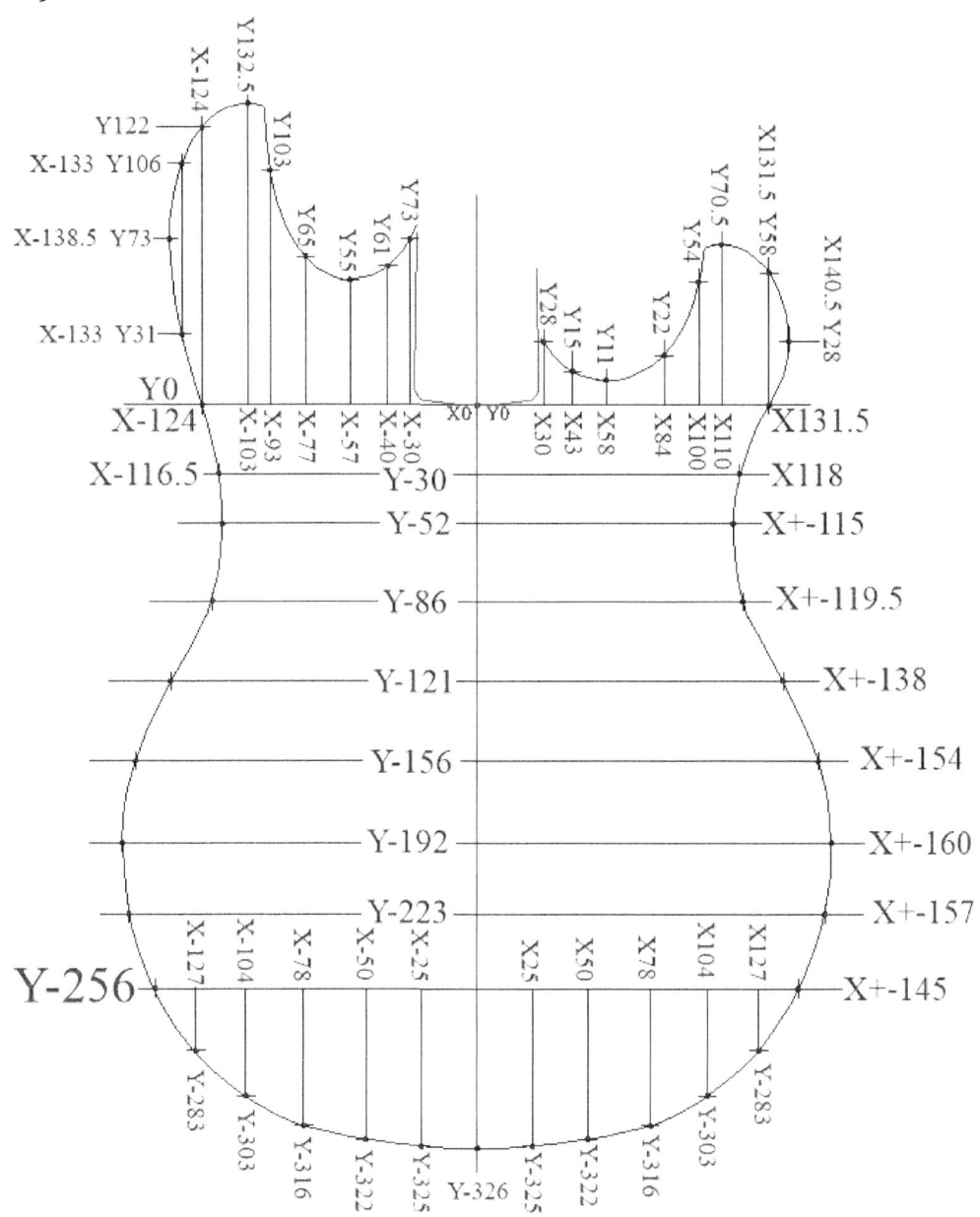

Mark the many points around the perimeter of Sides A. Draw smooth curves through these points. Take great care that the curves are smooth and continuous. View the curves from the front and from the back which is free of markings.

Other laminates can be later marked by simply copying around the curves of Sides A.

7.3) Mark-out the Interior of Sides A

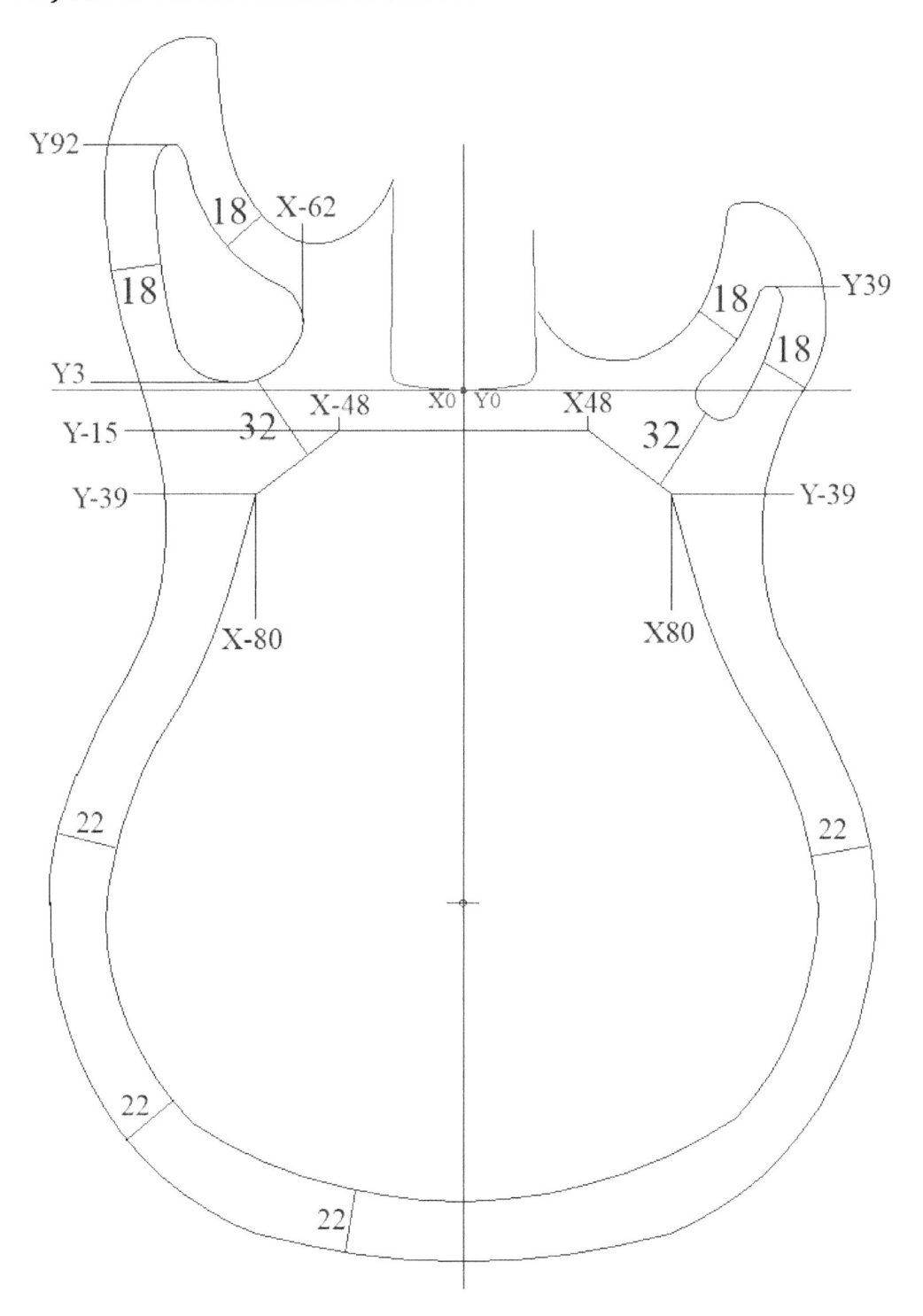

Page 51

7.4) Saw Out the Perimeter of Sides A

Use your scroll saw or coping saw to cut out the outside of Sides A. Do the final smooth curve shaping with a fine rasp or with rough sandpaper.

7.5) Saw Out the Insides of Sides A

Drill an 8mm = 5/16in hole in each of the inside cut-outs. Undo the top of the saw blade and fit it through the hole. Saw each cut-out.

7.6) If Needed, Thicken Sides A with Sides B

Sides AB can be made of a single piece of 18mm = 3/4in plywood.

Alternatively you can screw and glue together:

9mm + 9mm or A 12mm + B 6mm.

3/8in + 3/8in or A 1/2in + B 1/4in.

B is an exact copy of A, marked by drawing around A as a template.

Use the same screw positions as Sides D so that screws of Sides C will not hit these Sides B screws.

7.7) Ensure That the Neck Will Fit Perfectly

Test your neck in the neck pocket. Sand the pocket to shape if need. Do not sand the neck heel, assuming it is a correct width 2 3/16 in wide = 55.6mm. Make sure that you sand the sides of the pocket square to the front surface. It is quite easy to do this at this stage. If you wait until Sides C is added, the neck pocket will have a back, as well as sides, and will be a lot more difficult to work on.

7.8) Rasp the Chamfer of Sides A

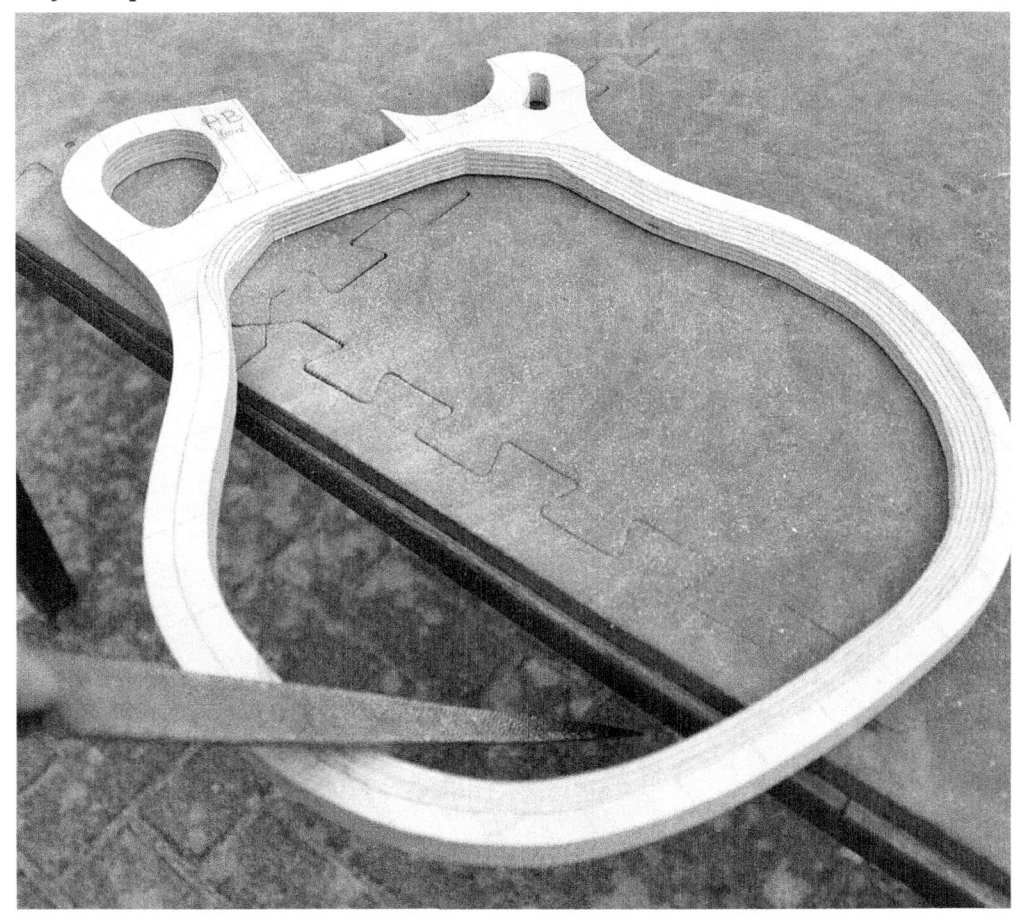

Sides A has an 11mm chamfer around it's front inside. This is so as to maximise the free soundboard area. It allows the sides to be 22mm thick for great stiffness and tuning stability. Cut this chamfer with a rasp, and finish it with rough sandpaper. Near the neck pocket the chamfer is reduced to 2mm.

8) Make the Front Soundboard

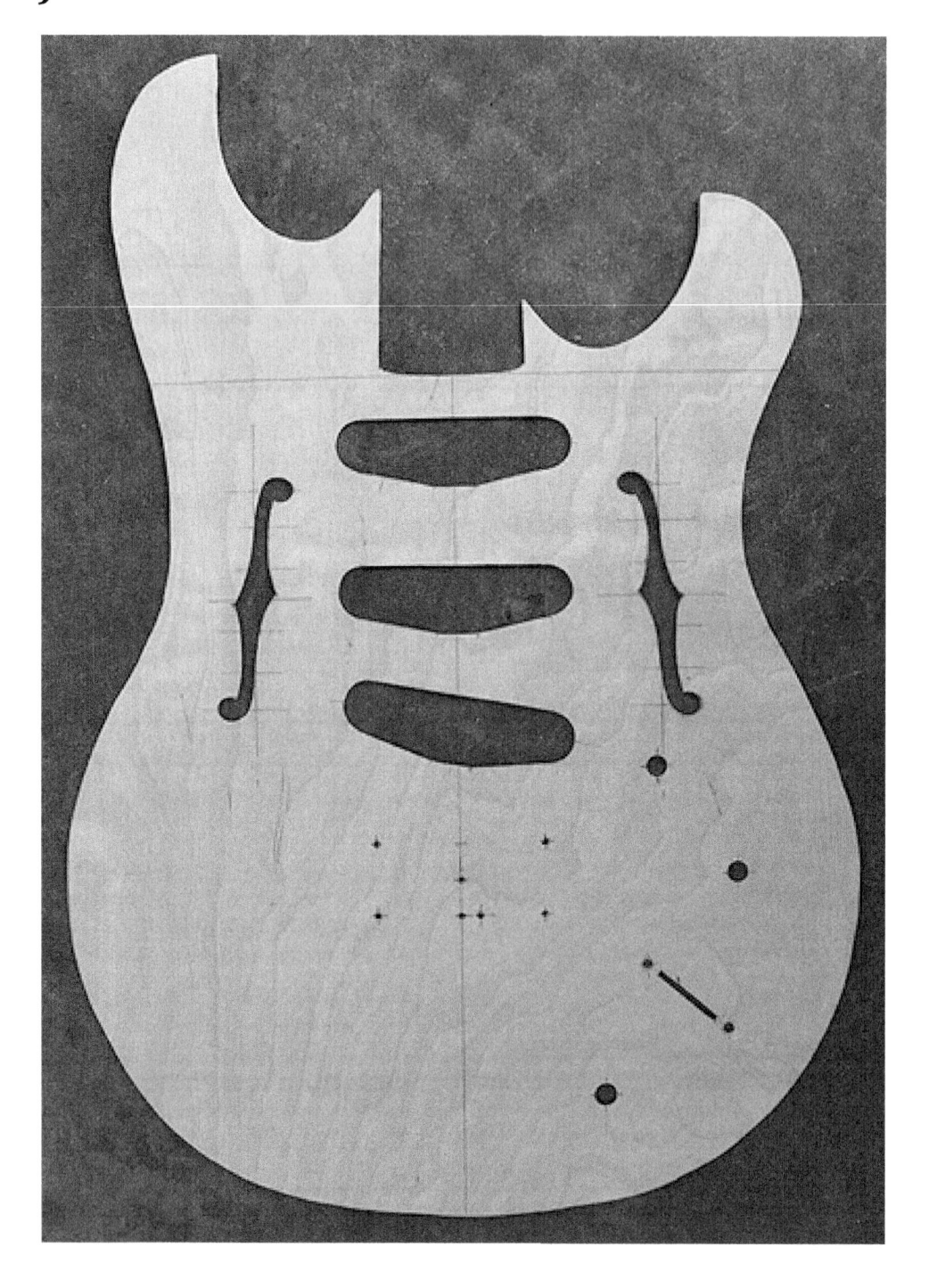

8.1) Copy Sides AB Outline onto Front Soundboard

Use Sides AB as a template to draw the outline of the front soundboard. This should have the whole perimeter and the neck pocket.

8.2) Mark-out the XY Coordinate Lines

Firstly, position the centre line. Mark the centre of the neck pocket. The centre should be 27.8mm from each side of the neck pocket. Mark the centre of the rump of the guitar. The widest part is 320mm = +-160mm. Draw the centre line between the two marks.

Secondly, position the Y0 datum line. This crosses the centre line at right-angles, at the inside end of the neck pocket. Use a set square and ruler to position this line.

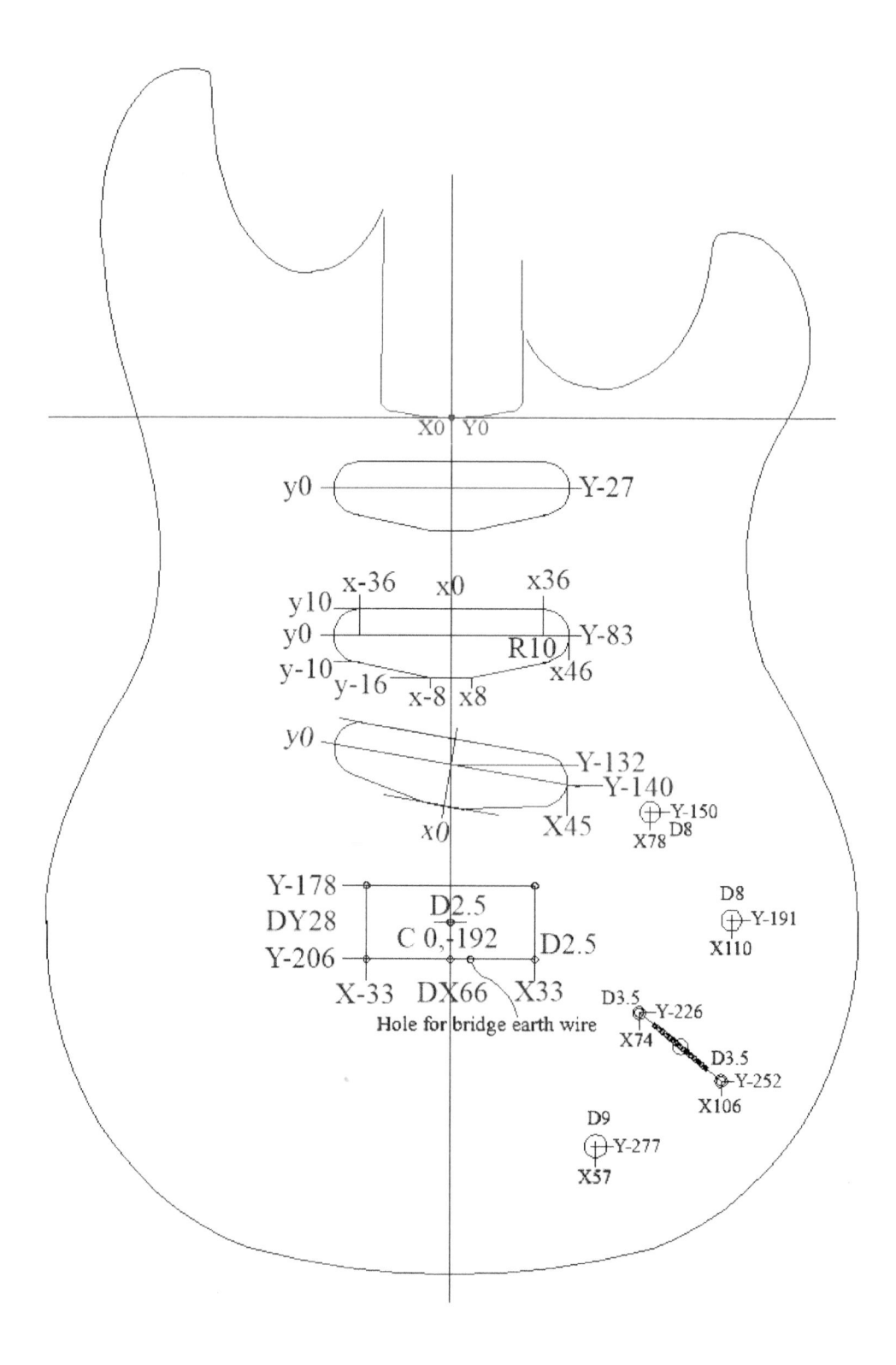

8.3) Mark-out the Bridge Screw-Holes

The strat top-loader bridge is screwed on with 5 screws as dimensioned.

Mark a hole for the bridge earth wire, a bit to one side of the middle bridge screw hole.

Mark a 2.5mm = 3/32in alignment hole at the centre of the bridge Y-192. This hole will line up with one on the struts, and the bridge block, to provide accurate alignment of the parts from front to back.

8.4) Mark-out the Pickup Holes

All three pickup holes are the same size and shape. They are shifted, and one is rotated. Their absolute positions are given with X and Y coordinates. The shape of a pickup uses local coordinates x and y from the middle of the pickup.

8.5) Mark-out the Control Holes

The 5 way pickup selector is positioned by the two screw holes. Mark the centre line of the blade switch between the two screw holes. Then mark the blade slot being 2mm wide.

8.6) Mark-out the Front Soundboard F-Holes

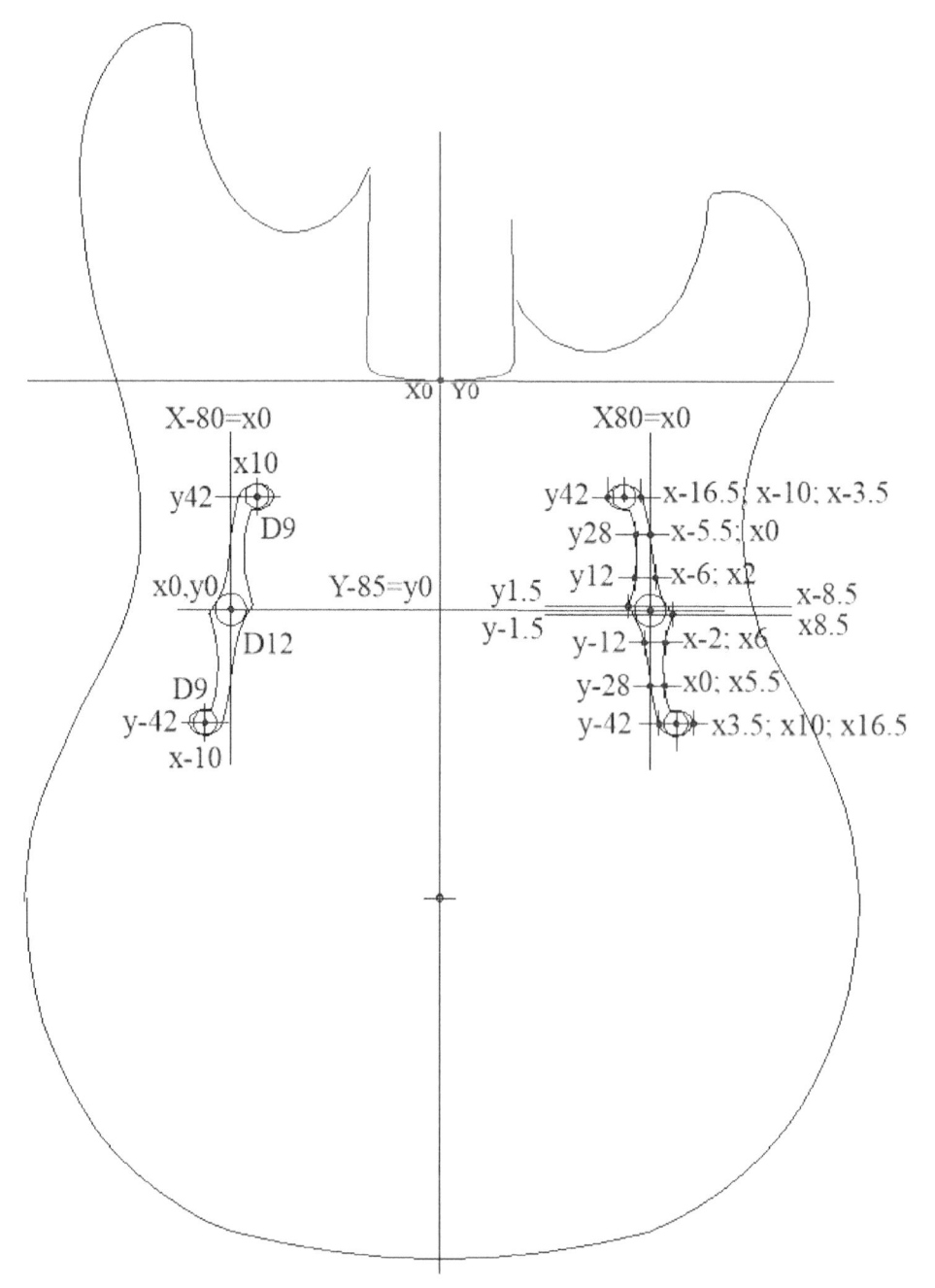

X-80=x0
x10
y42
D9
x0,y0
Y-85=y0
D12
D9
y-42
x-10

X0 Y0

X80=x0
y42 x-16.5; x-10; x-3.5
y28 x-5.5; x0
y12 x-6; x2
y1.5   x-8.5
y-1.5   x8.5
y-12 x-2; x6
y-28 x0; x5.5
y-42 x3.5; x10; x16.5

Both f holes are the same size and shape, being mirror-images from the centre. Their absolute positions are given with X and Y coordinates. The shape of both f holes uses local coordinates x and y from the middle of the f hole.

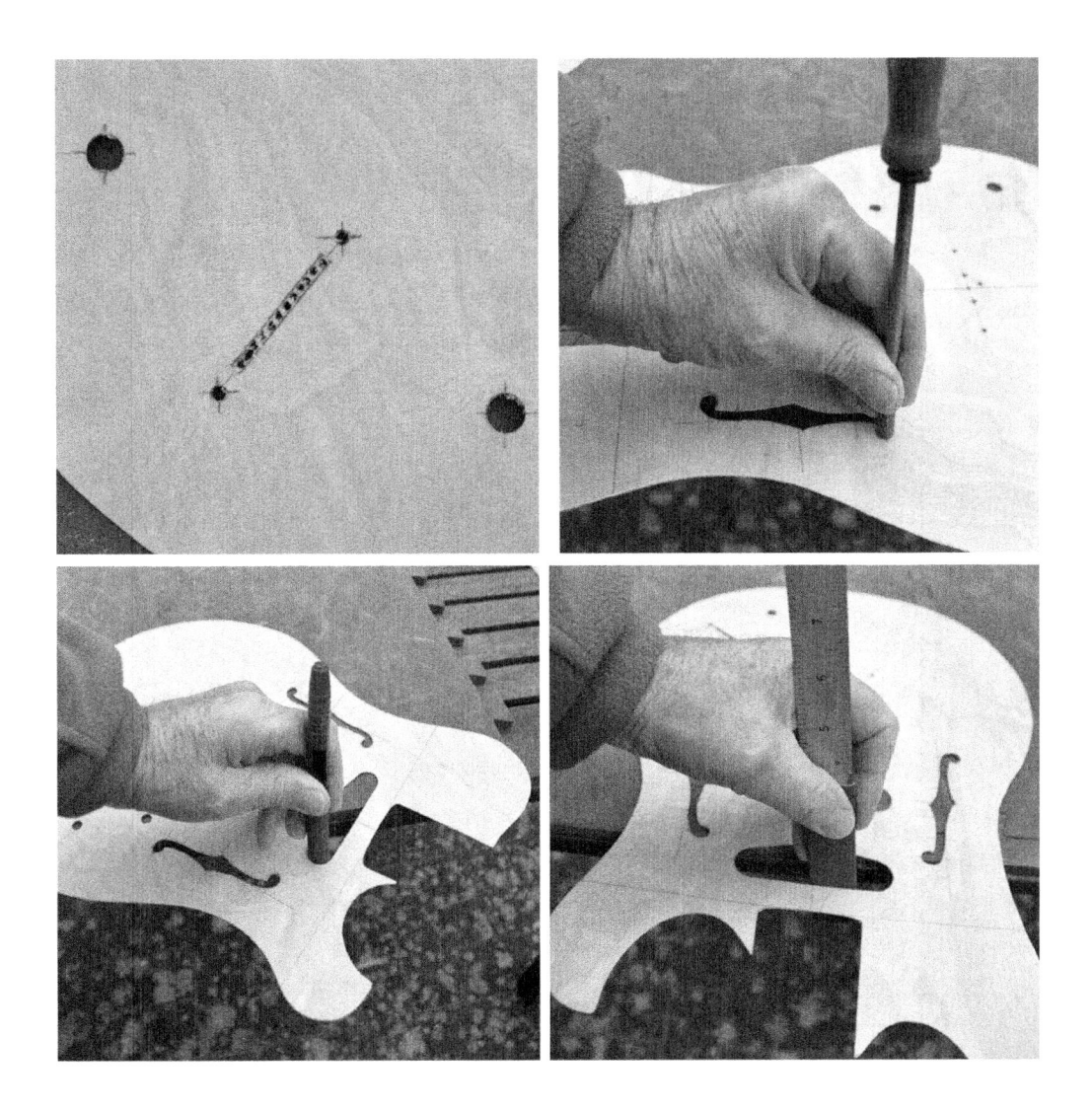

8.7) Sawing the Front Soundboard

Go gently with a fine new sharp saw blade. Cosmetics are important on this one. Support the plywood firmly on the flat surface while cutting in order to minimise splintering.

8.8) Drilling the Front Soundboard

It is delicate, go through slowly, and exit the hole very gently. You must use your proper sharp 8mm = 5/16in wood-drill for large holes. Common twist drills are OK for small holes, and must be sharp to avoid splintering. Always hold the soundboard firmly onto a clean flat piece of scrap wood to prevent back splintering.

8.9) Cutting a Slot for the 5 Way Selector

This might be the most tricky part of this guitar build.

Drill the two fixing holes as accurately as possible. Start with 2mm or 1/16in drill and finish with 3.5mm or 1/8in drill

Check that they have exactly the right span against your selector switch.

   If not, slot just one hole a little longer, and not wider, with a folded rough sandpaper, or a round needle file.

Check that your slot mark-out is exactly between the two actual holes.

   If not, rub out the mark-out with rubber or medium sandpaper,

     and mark it again along the middle of the actual hole positions.

Drill out the slot with many cuts from a 1.5mm = 1/16in drill. See the photo above.

Cut the many tiny holes into one long slot. You can use a sharp knife carefully. Better still, you can use a short piece of broken hack-saw blade.

Finish the slot with rough sandpaper.

8.10) Sanding the Front Soundboard Cut-outs

Use a medium sandpaper e.g. 120P grit. Use a ruler to hold the sandpaper flat along the straight edges of the pickup holes. Wrap the sandpaper around a suitable size cylinder object to sand the rounded parts.

Use a 15mm by 60mm strip of sandpaper to sand the edges of the f holes. Place the front soundboard flat on the edge of a table. Put the sandpaper strip half way though the f-hole. Hold the sandpaper tight between fingers and thumbs, one hand above and one hand below the f-hole.

9) Make the Struts for the Soundboard

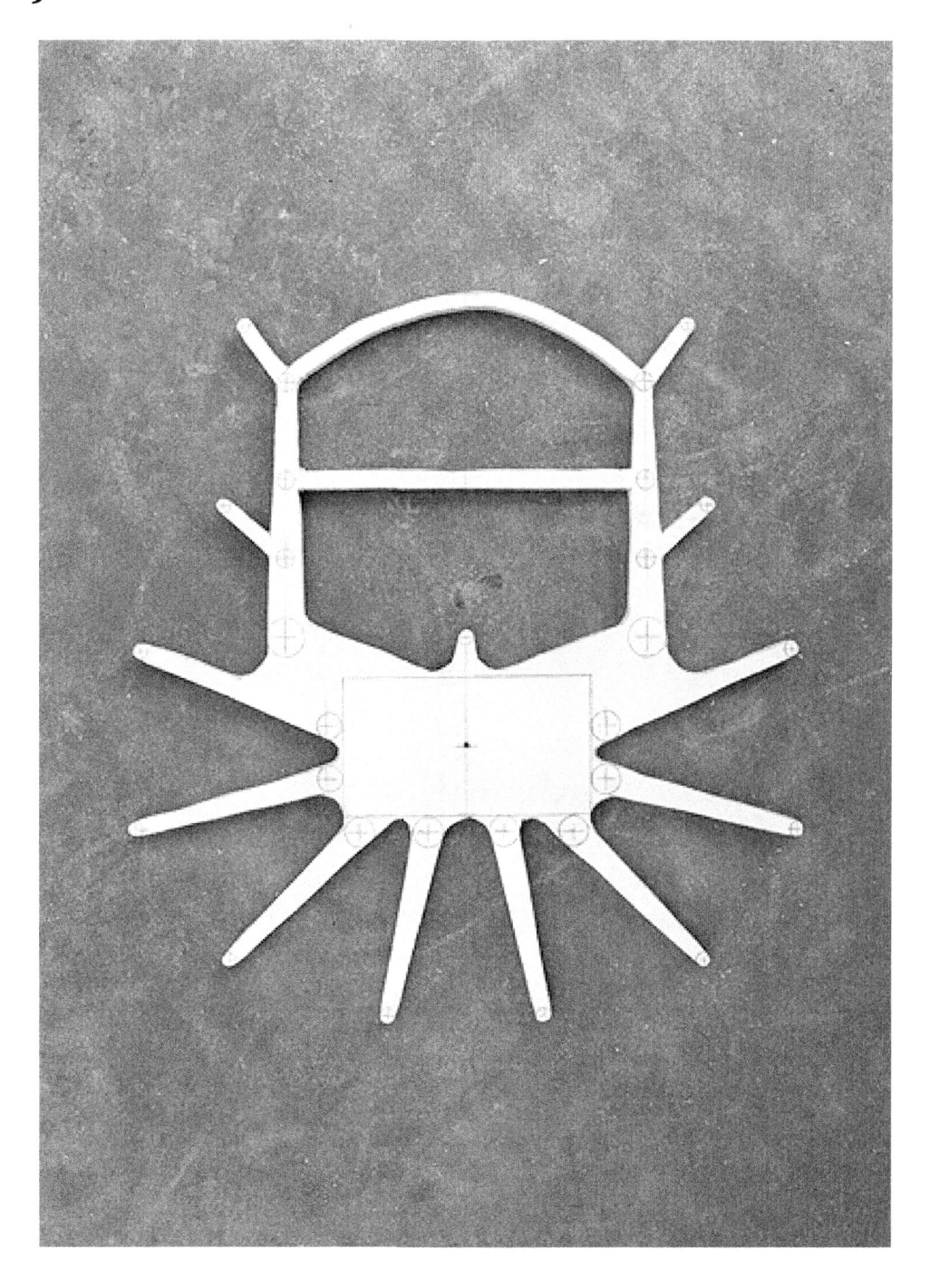

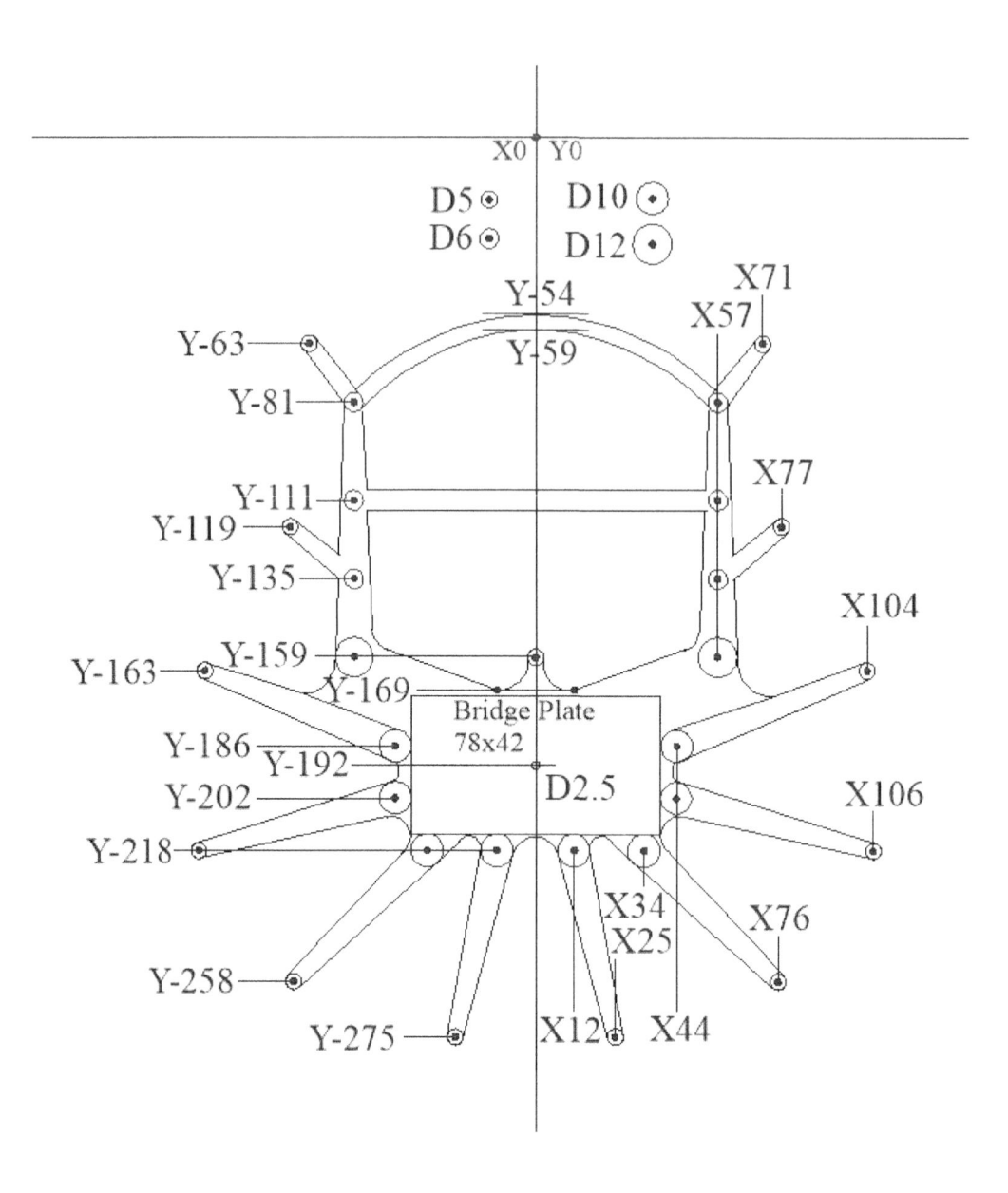

9.1) Mark Out the Struts

The struts are symmetric left to right, so you can not glue it on the wrong way round. They are made of 6mm = ¼ in plywood. Draw the X and Y coordinate lines at right angles to one another. Draw all the marker circles at the shown coordinate positions: 2 off D12; 8 off D10 around the bridge plate; 6 off D6 on the long arms; 12 off D5 at the outer ends of struts.

Draw the bridge plate position and the bridge centre alignment hole, both centred at Y-192.

9.2) Cut Out the Struts

Saw out the struts with your scroll saw or coping saw.

Rough sand all edges of the struts.

10) Glue the Struts Inside the Soundboard

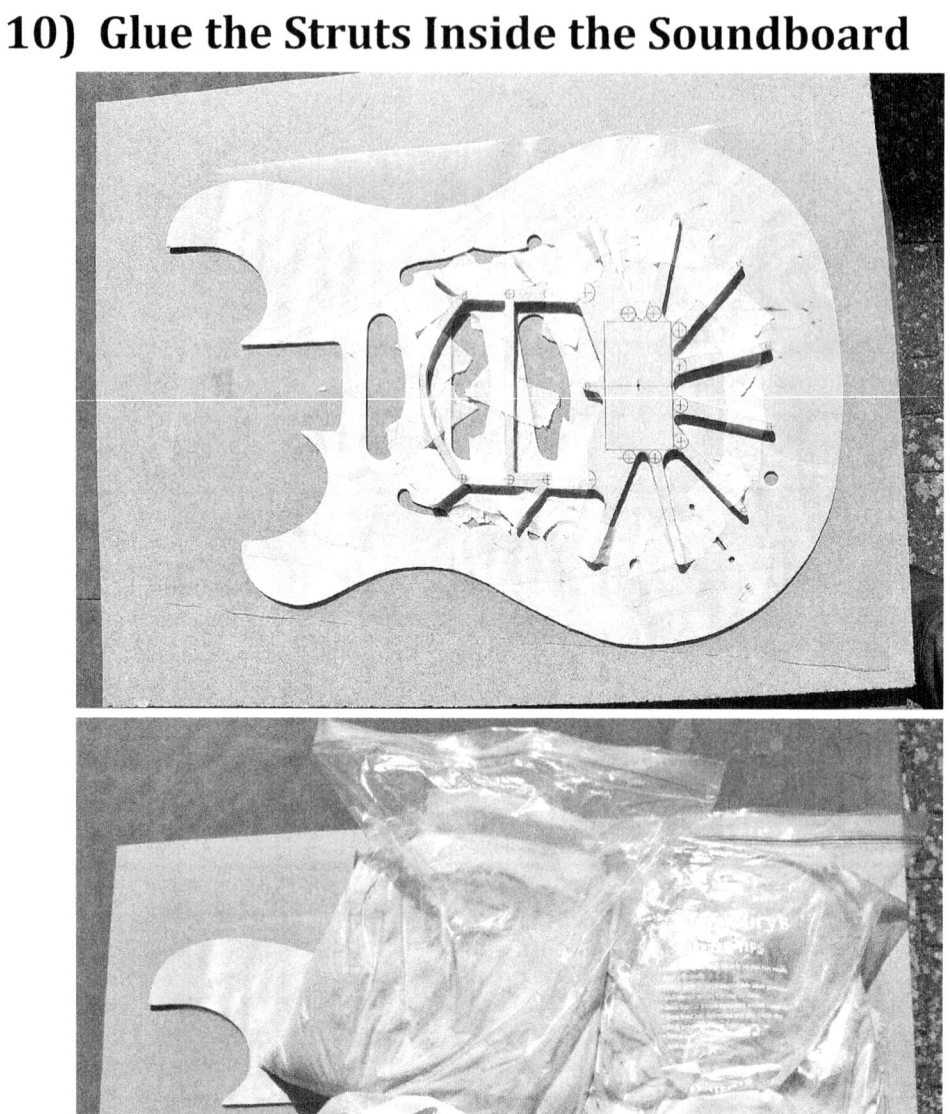

10.1) Mark the Position of the Struts

It is important that the bridge, the soundboard, the struts, and the bridge back block, all align correctly. To facilitate that, there is a 2.5mm construction hole at X0 Y-192 which marks the centre of the bridge parts. Place a temporary 2mm twist drill through the holes to align the struts on the inside of the front soundboard. Rotate the struts to line up the centre lines. The struts should be centred between the f-holes. Draw the outline of the struts onto the soundboard

10.2) Glue and Tape the Struts

Perform this assembly on a flat surface, covered in a sheet of polythene, to prevent any accidental glue sticking it down. Spread white glue within the outline on the soundboard inside. Spread glue on the front surface of the struts. Join them together. Check the alignment with a 2mm twist drill in the 2.5 mm alignment holes. Use removable masking tape to hold all parts of the struts flat, in the right position, on the soundboard.

10.3) Use Sandbags to Hold the Assembly Flat

During the glue drying time of several hours, all parts of the struts must be held firmly flat on the soundboard. This might require about 25 conventional small clamps at considerable cost. A much easier, and completely reliable, method of clamping is to use gravity! Fill some polythene freezer bags with heavy play-sand. Place them over the assembly. Gently massage them with your hands so that the weight of the sand is pressing evenly on top of every part of the struts.

Leave the assembly undisturbed overnight. The next day remove the sand bags and remove the tape. The soundboard should then be stiff and flat.

10.4) Tune the struts

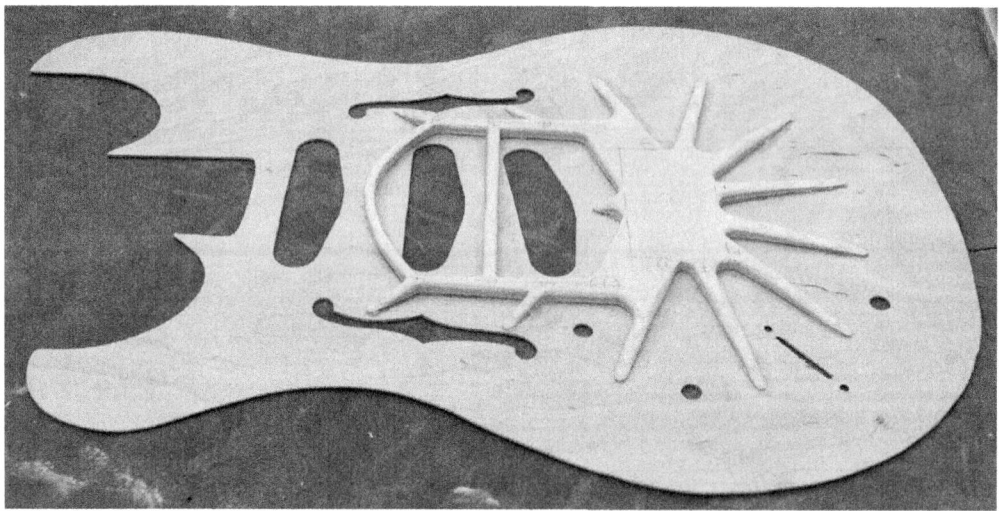

Place the soundboard on a soft flat surface. Foam or carpet, so that the front surface does not get scratched.

The struts must be shaped so that they are progressively stiff near the bridge, to flexible near the perimeter. This strutted soundboard then works like an amplifier loudspeaker, projecting crisp bright treble from its centre, and deep full bass from its outer large area. Each strut should be thinned so that they are 6mm = 1/4 in thick near the bridge, tapering down to 1.5mm = 1/16 in at the end.

Each strut should be slightly rounded and smoothed.

A very sharp chisel is the ideal tool for thinning and shaping the struts. Alternatively, use a very sharp knife. You could do it all with rough sandpaper on a sanding block. Sanding it all is fairly easy, but takes a longer time. Take care not to sand the main soundboard surface.

Cut away from you and away from the bridge. Beware slips, splits, and splintering: never place your holding hand in front of the chisel or knife.

11) Glue the Sides AB onto the Front Soundboard

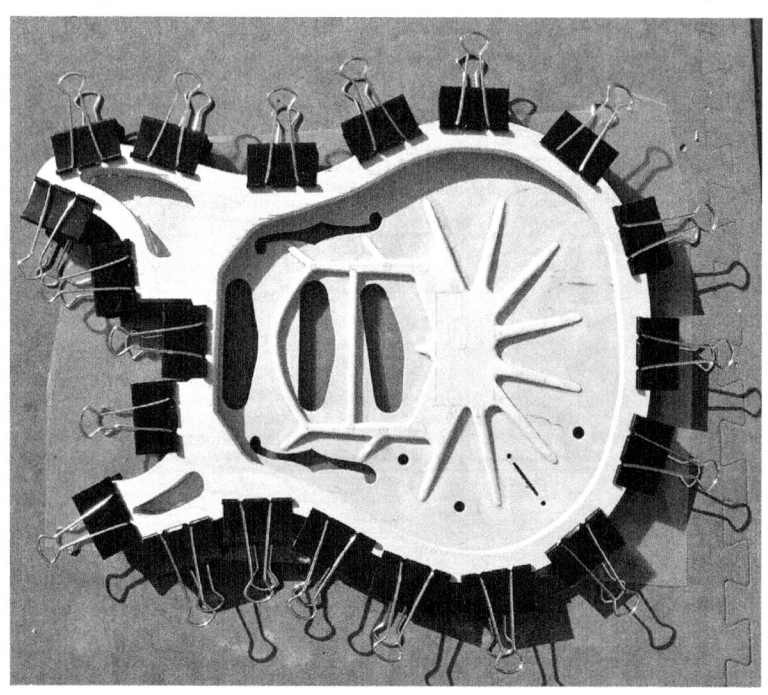

Page 68

11.1) Glue Together

The Sides AB are glued onto the front soundboard. Assemble on a flat surface, with a polythene sheet to prevent anything sticking onto it. Screws can not be used as the soundboard is thin. You would not want visible screws around the front. Apply glue to both surfaces and join together. Slide the two parts together in perfect alignment. Use 2 in = 52mm bulldog clips as clamps. You will need about two dozen. First clamp one by the neck pocket, then one opposite at the middle of the rump. Adjust the alignment if needed while releasing one or the other clip. Add 2 more clips spread out on each side. Ad clips all around, so that every part of the join is clamped firmly. If you were to use insufficient glue, or insufficient clamping, you could get a disastrous dry joint which might rattle. Scrape excess glue off before it dries. Leave clamped overnight while the glue sets.

11.2) Shape Up

Next day, remove all clips. Rasp and rough sand this body-front-half. Perfect the curves of the perimeter. This will be the final beautiful shape of your guitar. Take care to keep the sides of the guitar square to the front.

11.3) Use as a Template to Mark All Other Layers

Place this body-front-half on each in turn of: Sides C; Sides D; Back Cover. Mark out the perimeter of each by drawing around it.

11.4) Mark-out the XY Coordinate Lines on Every Layer

Firstly, position the centre line. Mark the centre of the neck pocket. The centre should be 27.8mm from each side of the neck pocket. Mark the centre of the rump of the guitar. The widest part is 320mm = +-160mm. Draw the centre line between the two marks.

Secondly, position the Y0 datum line. This crosses the centre line at right-angles, at the inside end of the neck pocket. Use a set square and ruler to position this line.

12) Add Sides C and D to the Body

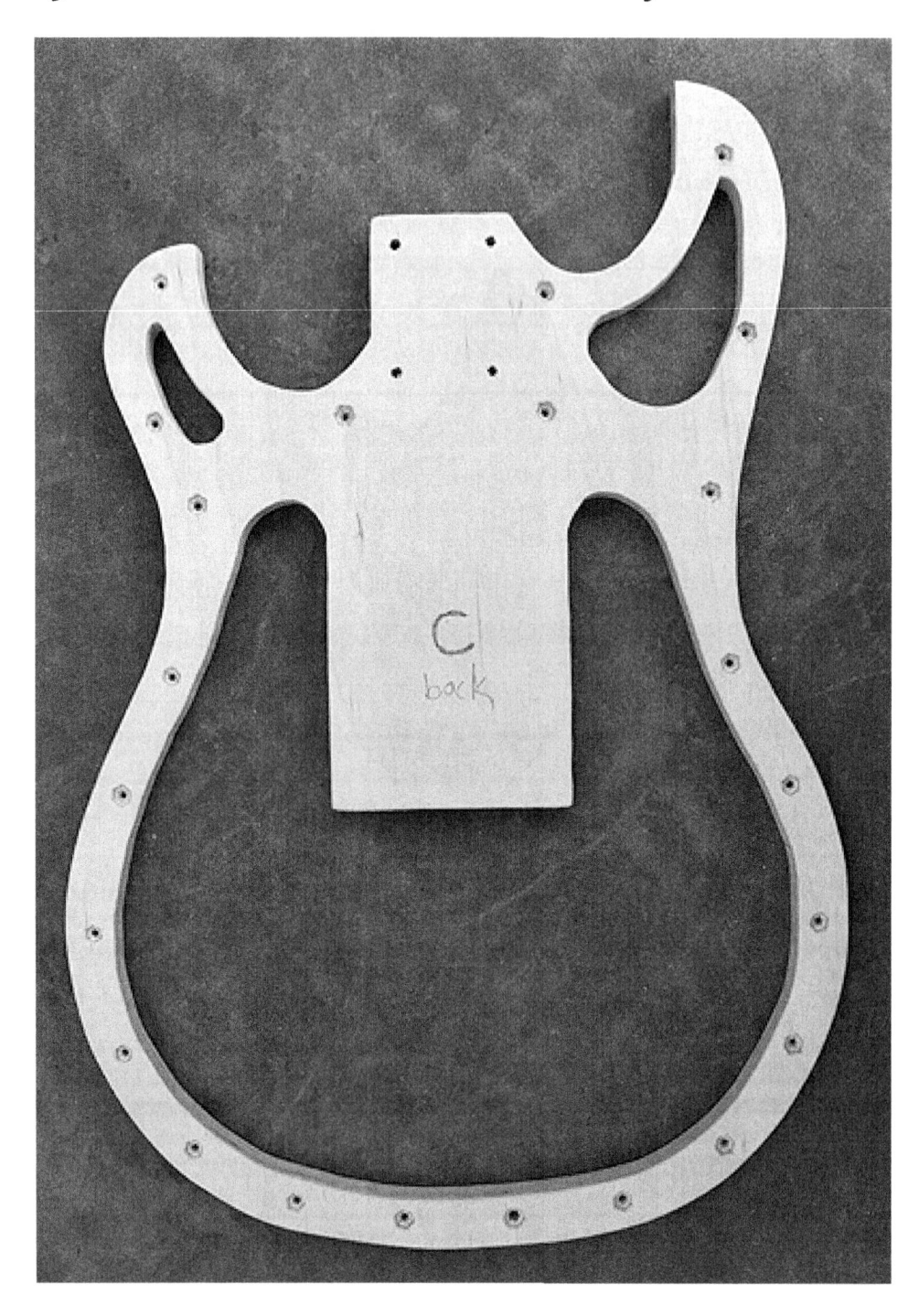

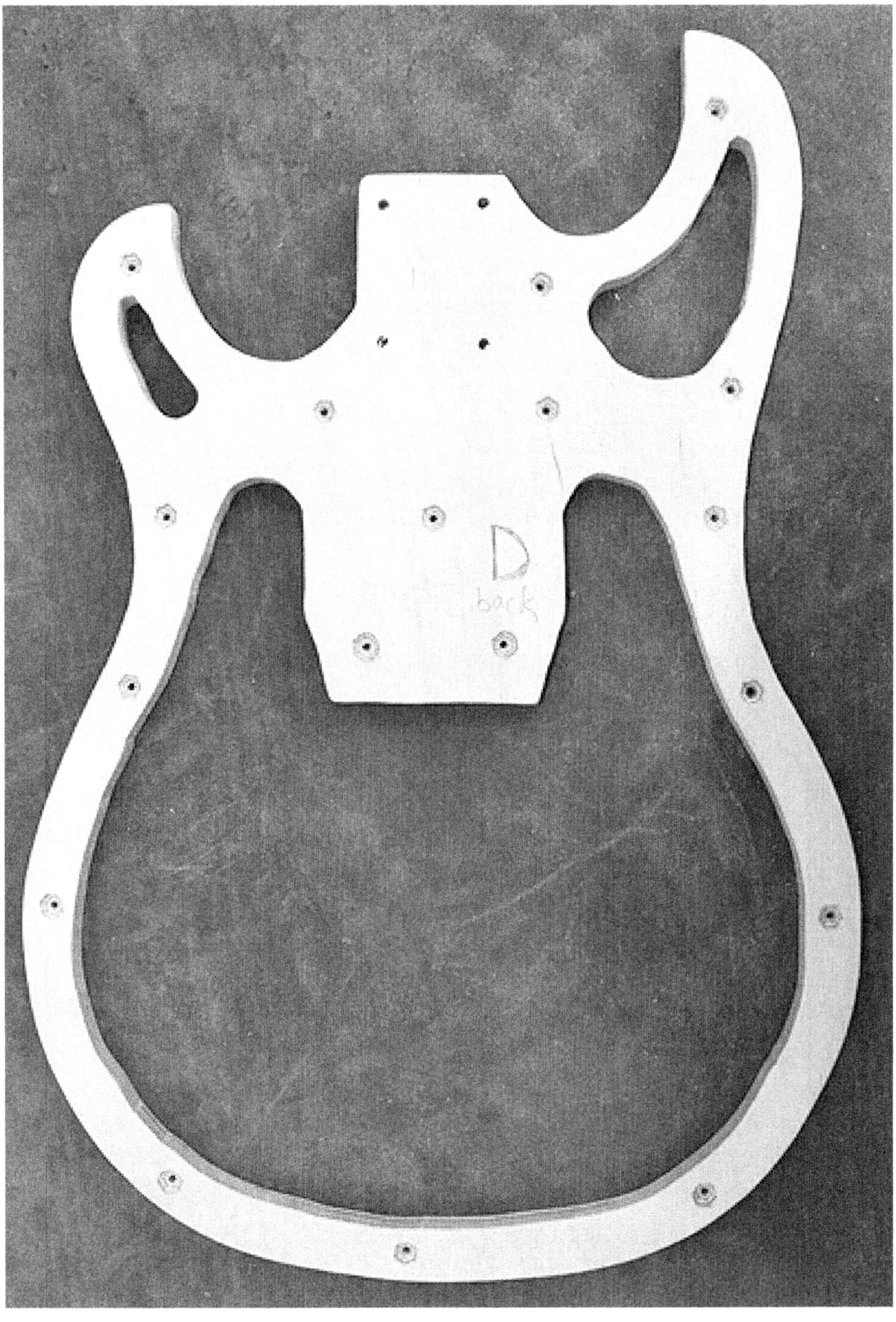
D
back

12.1) Add Sides C, with glue and screws

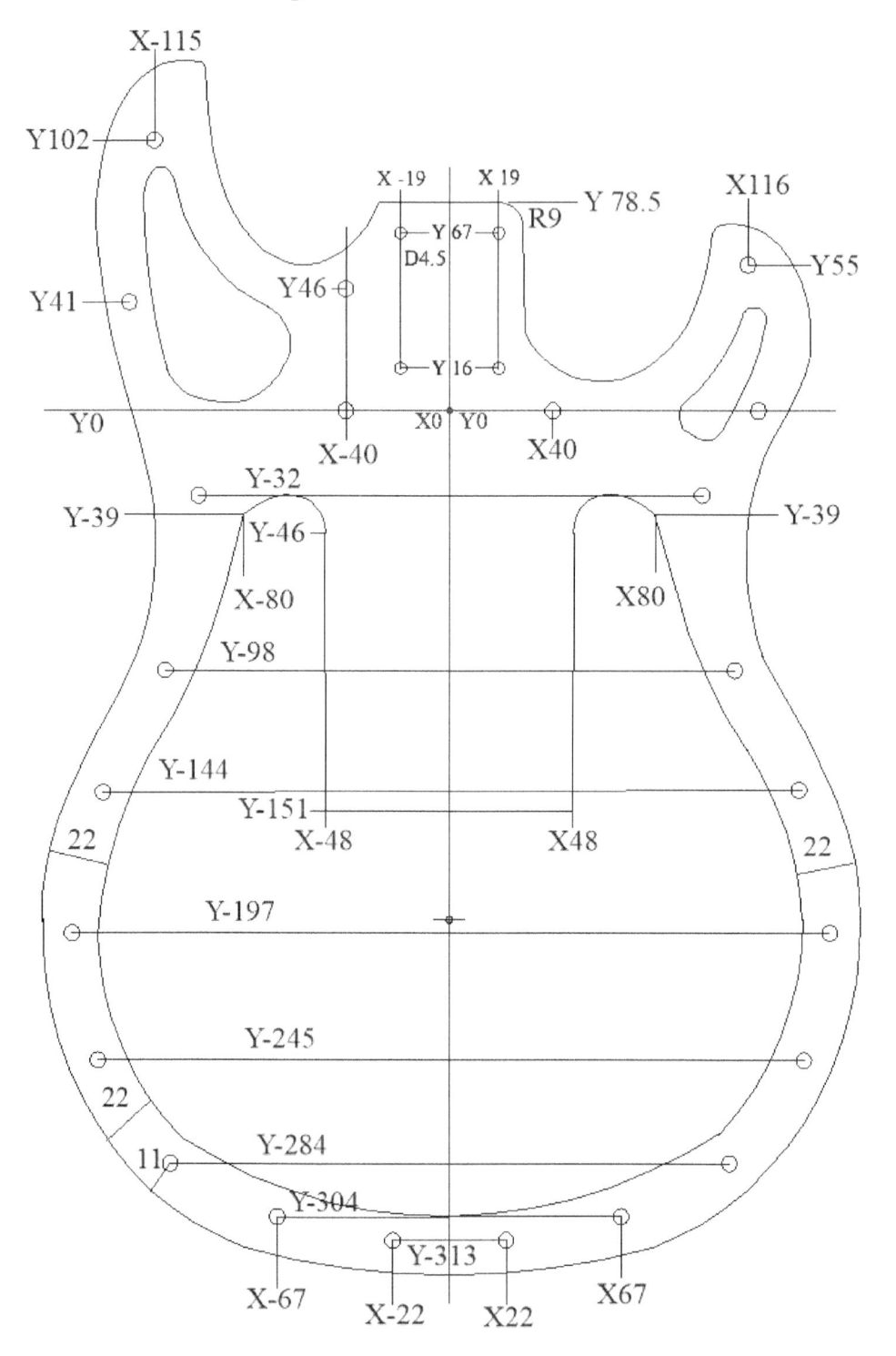

12.2) Add Sides D, with glue and screws

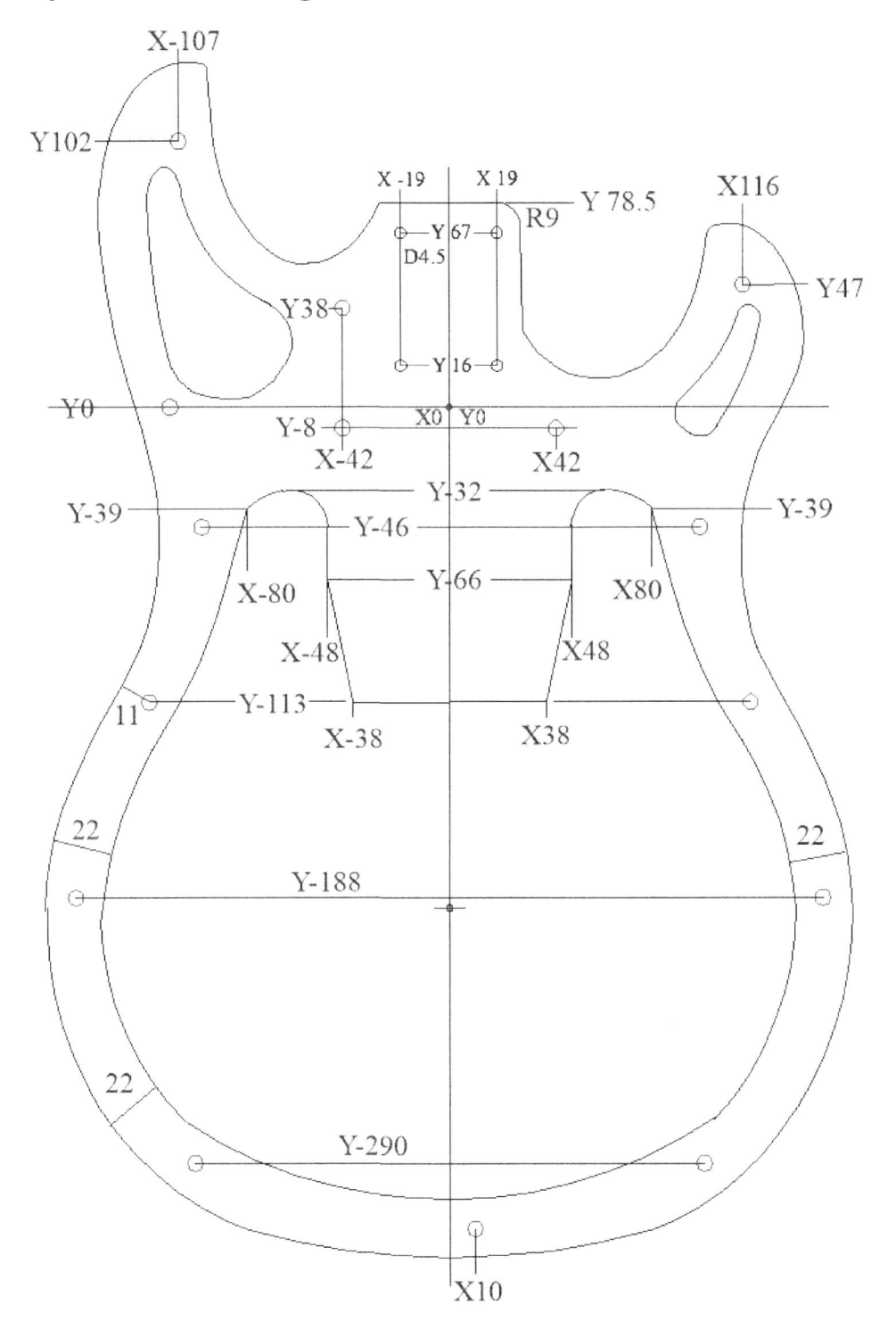

Most of the outlines and inner lines can be copied using Sides AB as a template. The central spine of the guitar is different in Sides C and Sides D.

Note that each layer of the sides has it's screw holes at alternatives of two sets of positions. This is so that the screws of one layer do not crash into the screws of the previous layer.

Use No4 x 3/4in = M3mm x 18mm screws to join Sides C to Sides AB; then Sides D to Sides C.

The screw holes should be drilled 3mm = 1/8 in. Then the countersinks should be drilled on the side which is nearest the back of the guitar. The countersinks should be just deep enough to completely bury the screw heads.

Align the two parts without glue. Drill 2mm = 5/64 in for the full length of the screw ¾ in = 18mm. Do two opposite screw holes first, screw together and check alignment. Drill and screw all. Undo; glue up; screw all.

13) Make the Body Back Cover

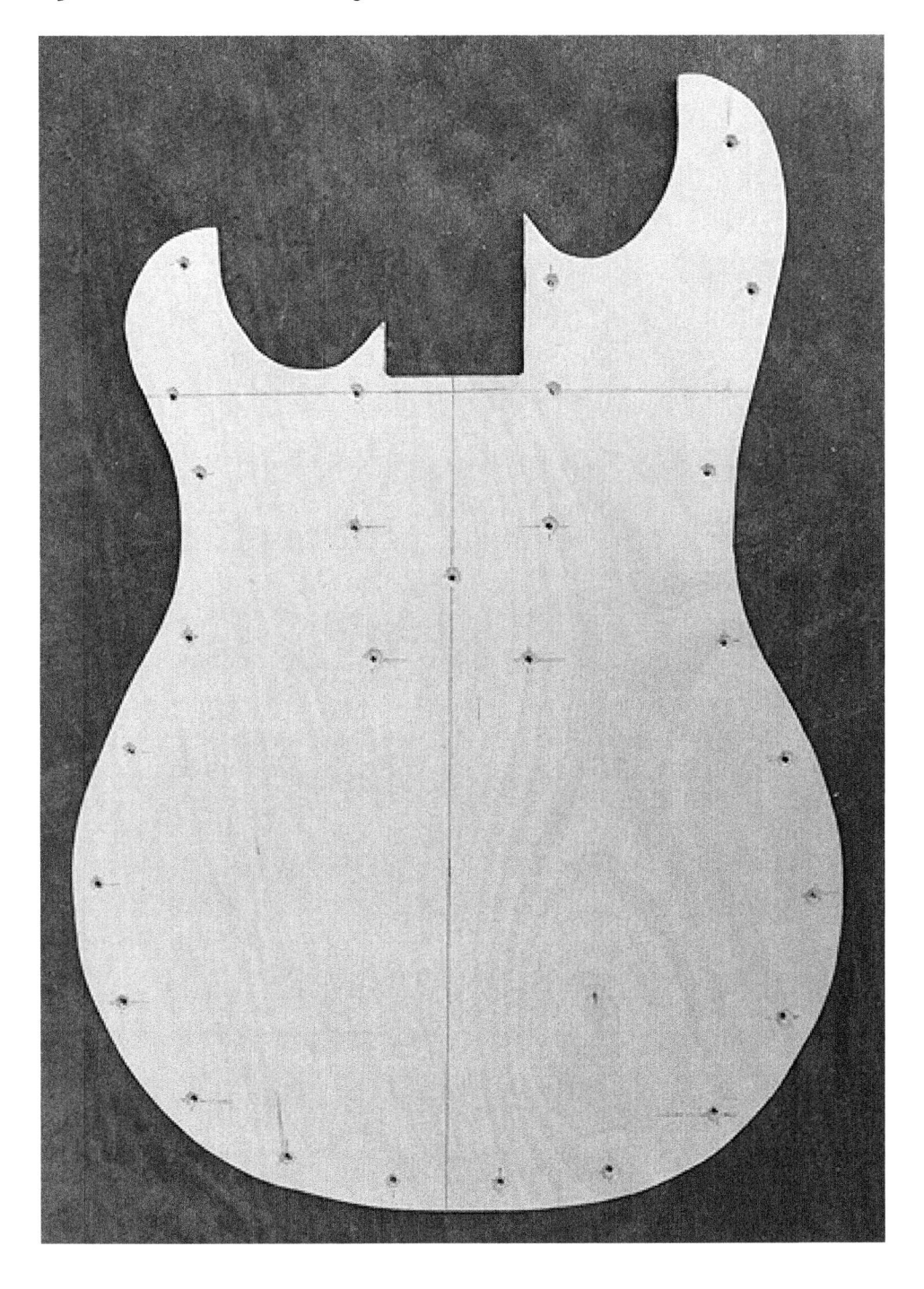

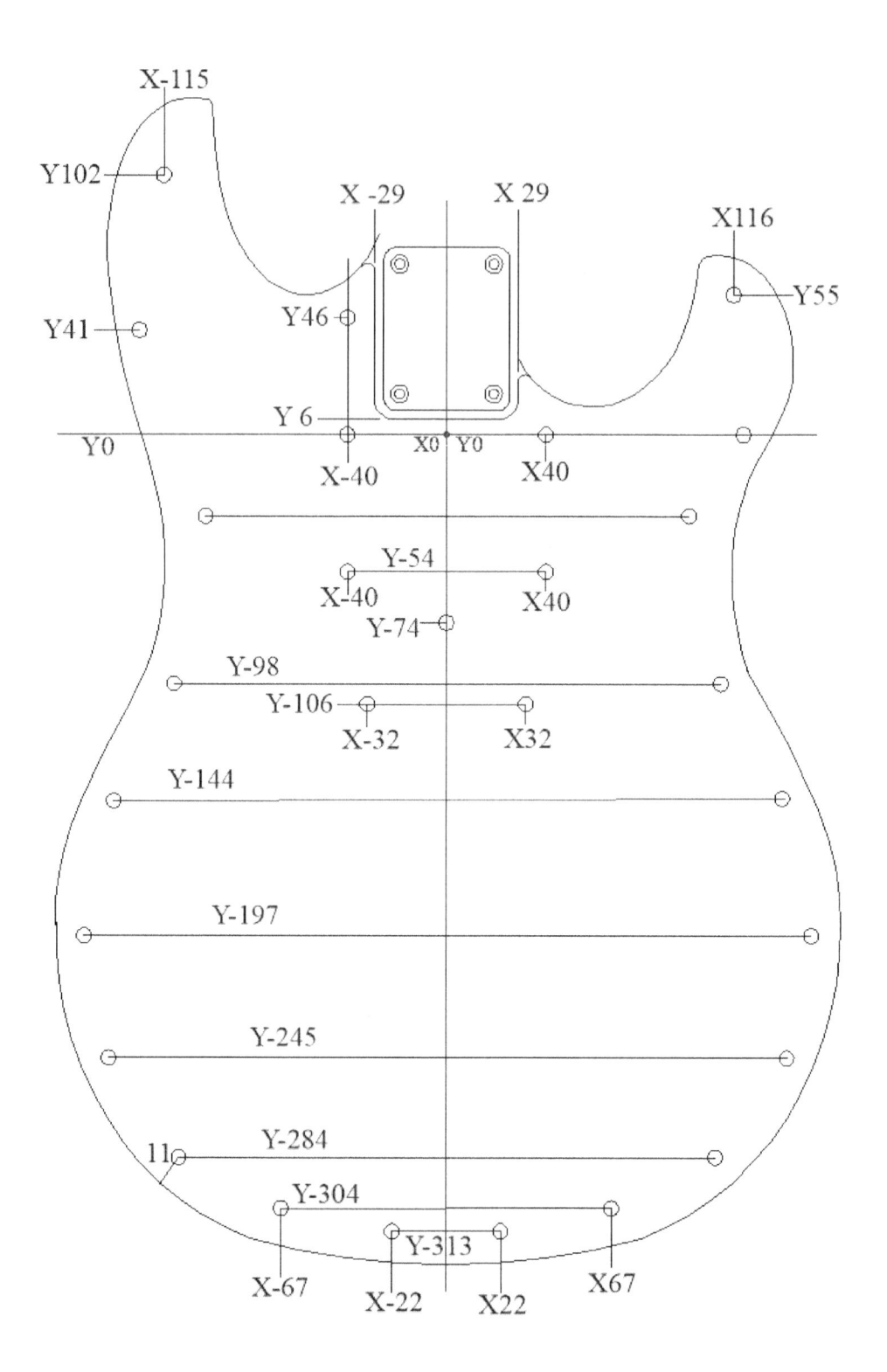

13.1) Mark-out Back Cover

Use the currently assembled body as a template, draw around it onto the 3mm =1/8 in back cover. Mark-out the centre line and the Y0 line.

There is a cut-out around the neck plate at a safe distance. This has squared sides and rounded corners. This is not exactly the same as the neck pocket on the front and side layers.

13.2) Cut-out Back Cover

Use coping saw or scroll saw. Cut slowly with a sharp blade for a clean splinter-free result. All back side edges should be rounded with rough sandpaper then smoothed with medium then fine sandpaper.

13.3) Drill Screw Holes

The back cover is intended to be removable and replaceable, in order to give wide unrestricted access to all electronic components and wiring. Take care in the accuracy of the drilling, so that screws can be reused several times in the same holes, without stripping threads. Screws to be used are No4 x 1/2in = M3mm x 12mm. They require 3mm = 1/8 in holes through the back cover, and to be drilled at 2mm = 5/64 in into the body for the length of the screw.

13.4) Drill Countersinks

Countersinks to exactly cover the screw-heads should be drilled on the back side of the back cover. Make sure you recognise which side is which! Drill very gently to get the right depth. Practice a lot on scrap wood, until you have perfect control of depth and consistency of quality.

14) Make the Internal Bridge Mechanism

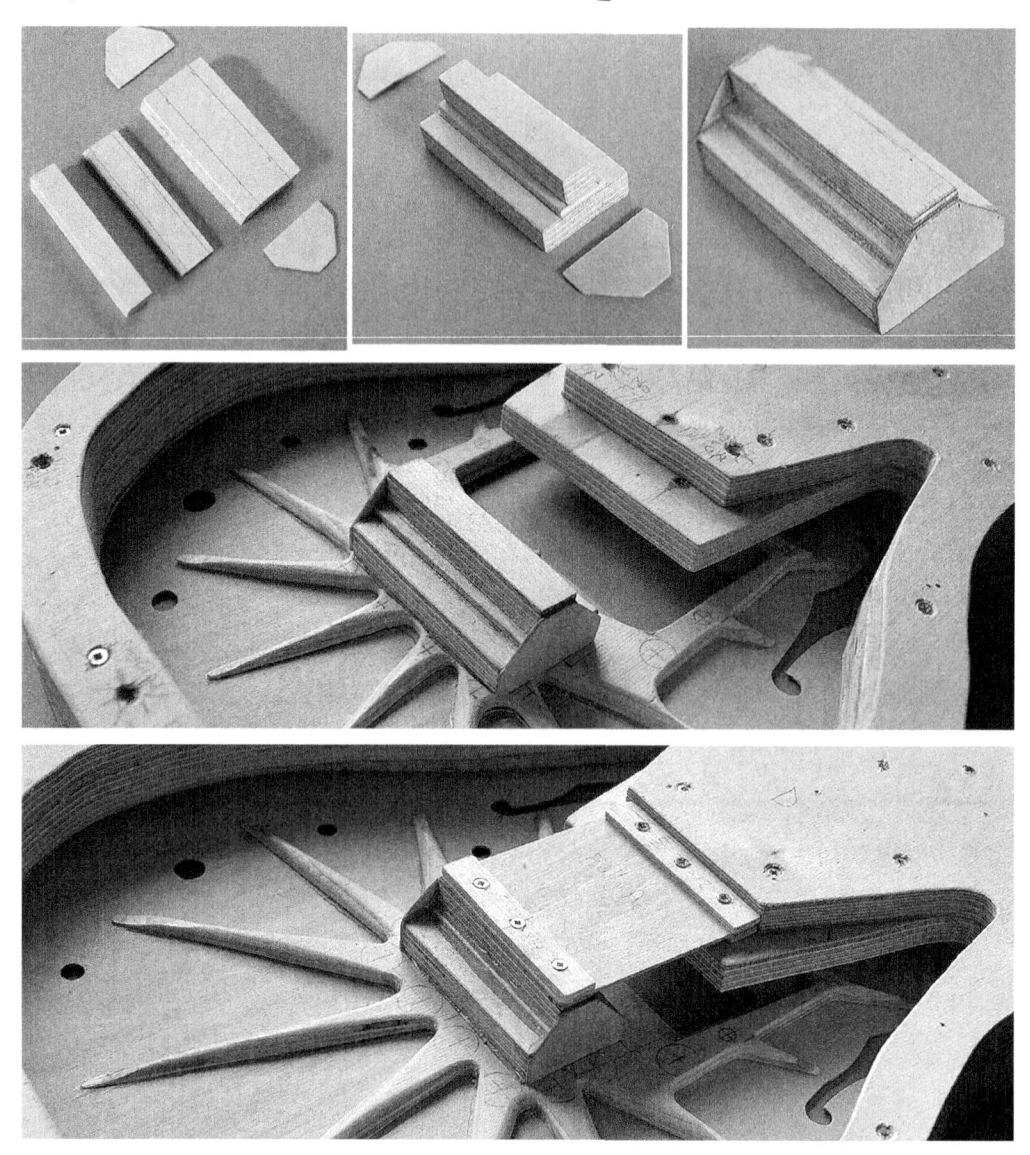

Page 78

14.1) Mark-out and Cut-out All Bridge Parts

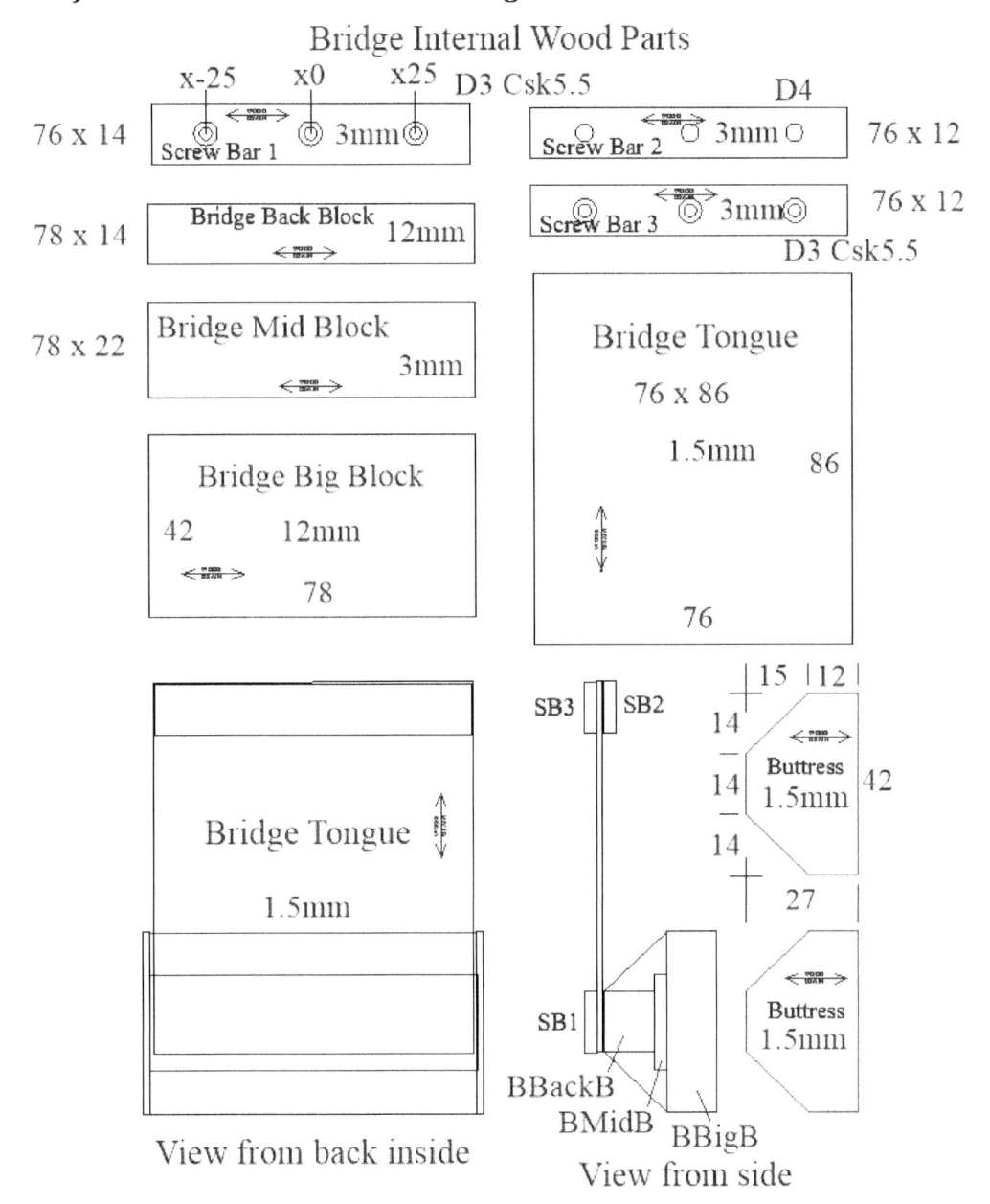

Bridge Internal Wood Parts

76 x 14 — Screw Bar 1: x-25, x0, x25, 3mm — D3 Csk5.5 — Screw Bar 2: 3mm — D4 — 76 x 12

78 x 14 — Bridge Back Block 12mm — Screw Bar 3: 3mm — 76 x 12 — D3 Csk5.5

78 x 22 — Bridge Mid Block 3mm

Bridge Big Block: 42, 12mm, 78

Bridge Tongue 76 x 86, 1.5mm, 86, 76

Buttress 1.5mm: 15, 12, 14, 14, 14, 42, 27

Bridge Tongue 1.5mm — View from back inside

SB3, SB2, SB1, BBackB, BMidB, BBigB — View from side

Buttress 1.5mm

14.2) Glue Together the Bridge Back Block

Use two-part quick set epoxy glue. This should set in 5 to 10 minutes, and is very strong. Parts can be simply held together while the glue sets, and do not need to be clamped. First glue together the Bridge Big Block and the Bridge Mid Block and the Bridge Back Block. Keep checking the alignment and gently pressing them together while the glue sets.

14.3) Glue the Buttresses onto the Block
Sand both ends of the bridge block, so that they are flat and square. Glue a buttress onto each end with quick epoxy. Optionally use a small screw to hold it on while the glue dries. Sand all edges of the assembly.

14.4) Glue the Bridge Block onto the Struts
Check that the position is correct with a quick dry assembly of the bridge block and bridge tongue. Screw Bar 1 caps the tongue onto the bridge block. At the neck end, Screw Bar 2 is a spacer below the tongue, and Screw Bar 3 caps the tongue.

Use quick epoxy to glue the bridge block onto the struts. Position the block carefully where you had marked it out accurately.

14.5) Glue and Screw On the Bridge Tongue
Screw everything together to make sure it all fits nicely. Unscrew, spread white glue on all contact surfaces, screw together.

15) Finishing the Wood Surfaces

Finishing the surfaces of the wood of guitars is a complicated art. Read this whole chapter carefully, before deciding which finish process will be best for your guitar. Practice to perfect your technique on scrap wood, before you commit to working on your guitar.

15.1) Guitars vs Furniture vs Buildings

Even the lowest cost factory made guitars have perfect finishes. The finish on a lot of furniture, and all wood parts of buildings, is of a lower standard because it needs to cover much larger areas quickly. So take great care and time when applying finishes to guitars. Viewers expect to see perfection, particularly on the front of the guitar.

If this is your first guitar build, then consider that a simple finish done well, will look better than an ambitious finish done badly.

If you aim to make a guitar that simply plays and sounds fantastic, and looks good, then choose a quick simple finishing process. If you want a most beautiful guitar, then allocate a long time to the finishing process.

15.2) Oil vs Lacquer vs Paint

Guitars are most commonly finished with paint for the mass-produced; lacquer for the more beautiful factory guitars; or oil for hand-made guitars.

Oils are completely transparent, and are used to bring out the natural beauty and figuring of the wood. They are often used without stains. Various wood-colour stains might be used on the wood, before applying the oil. Oils are easy to apply by hand. They are not very durable, but still look nice when old, as long as you like a well-played-in look.

Lacquers are of various types, of which each require very different applications, either brushing or spraying. The traditional 1950s guitar lacquer was nitro-cellulose. It looks nice, but a spilt glass of whisky will dissolve the lacquer off a guitar! It is dissolved in a toxic solvent, and needs to be sprayed, wearing protective gear, in a protective booth. The vapour of the solvent is bad for our global environment. Over several decades, other solvent-based polymer lacquers were developed, which offered more durable finishes. However they are still bad for the environment, and need to be sprayed. Over the past few years, excellent water-based polymer lacquers have been developed, that can be brushed, even indoors with no harm.

Paints are usually opaque, and provide even solid colours, in which you can not see the figuring of the wood. The most common paints are those used for spraying car bodies.

15.3) Compatible Stains

Avoid DIY shop finishes that sell as easy "stain and varnish all-in-one". They can look very good on a shed, or might be good on a house staircase, but would look very beginner DIY on a guitar.

It is safest to use a stain that remains completely stable throughout the finishing. The stain must not later re-dissolve, and uncontrollably spread around, when you apply the oil or lacquer. Oil and water do not mix, or dissolve in one another. If you finish with oil, then a water-based stain will be best. If you finish with water-based lacquer, then a spirit-based stain will be best. Test the compatibility of you finish choices, on a good sized piece of scrap wood, with curved edges, and rub a lot.

15.4) Make a Handle for the Body

A handle can be temporarily added to the body in the neck pocket. This is very useful to hold the body in one hand, and gives free access to all surfaces of the body, while applying finishes with your other hand.
See photo in paragraph 15.9)

Cut a piece of 18mm or 12mm plywood, 50mm wide and 200mm long. Drill four holes 3mm = 1/8 in at the neck screw positions. Drill an 8mm hole at the end of the handle so that the body can be hung on a hook while finishes dry. Use four neck screws to attach it.

Keep the back cover off the body throughout the finishing processes. Apply all finishes to the back cover in the same way as the front of the body. Also apply finishes around the sides of the body, and to the back of the neck joint.

15.5) Final Grain Raising and Fine Sanding

Before doing final sanding, raise the grain of the wood, by wetting the entire surface of the wood, with a brush or rag. This is quite an easy and exciting procedure. It takes 5 minutes to wet, then a half hour or an hour to dry.

Wetting first reveals the beauty of the markings of the wood. Curly grains look fantastic. It also reveals, while wet, any unwanted scratches in the wood surface. Carefully observe and remember where those demon scratches are, so that you can sand them out when the wood has dried.

If there are any deep scratches, you might rough sand them out while the wood is wet, then start again with grain raising wash.

I must stress the importance of perfect final sanding, particularly so if you are going to stain the wood. Use P240 grit sandpaper. Any tiny scratches, after the final sanding, will become horribly visible when stain is applied. Do all final fine sanding straight in the direction of the wood grain. Take extra care on the whole front of the guitar. That is what everybody looks at in detail.

Look very carefully at all the front outside edges of the body. The most common mistake is to leave some of the cross-grain deep scratches of the perimeter shaping, and edge rounding, still present on the edges of the front. If you find a few deep scratches you may need to go back to medium P120, then P180, sandpaper to eradicate them, then re-finish it with fine P240 sandpaper.

15.6) Simple Danish Oil Finish: Easiest

Work outdoors, or in a well ventilated shed. Wear rubber gloves. It is natural sticky stuff, not very bad for the environment. Dispose of used rags after they have dried out, away from buildings.

The easiest way to get a reliable good result, that avoids brush marks, is to rub Danish oil with a cotton cloth. Cut-up a cotton tee-shirt into 10cm or 5in patches. You do not need to use stains, but a very diluted stain before the oil can make the guitar a bit more beautiful. An oil finish is not as hard wearing as a lacquer or paint finish.

Day 1 (15 mins): Rub oil evenly with swirling round movements all over the surface of the front and sides of the body, and over the neck plate area of the back. Do the same on the back cover. Go over the whole surface twice. Dry for a day or more.

Day 2 (15 mins): Rub down gently with an abralon P600 abrasive pad. Be very gentle on edges and corners. Apply another layer of oil evenly with swirling round movements

Day 3 (10 mins): Apply another layer of oil, evenly with swirling round movements

Day 4 (15 mins): Rub down gently with an abralon P1000 abrasive pad. Be very gentle on edges and corners. Do all the rubbing in straight lines along the grain of the wood. Apply a final layer of oil, evenly in straight lines along the grain of the wood. Allow to dry and harden for several days or a week.

Several Days Later (10 mins): Buff up with a microfibre cleaning cloth. The more patient you were waiting for the oil to harden, the better the end result will be.

Extra coats of oil, and extra drying time between coats, both enhance the end result, if you have more time.

15.7) Other Oils

Linseed oil can look very good, and brings out the figuring of the wood very well. However it is very thin, and needs a lot more layers, and each layer takes many days to dry. In cold damp weather it just does not dry!

Tung Oil has more body, and works quite well. But it is more difficult to spread evenly, and requires more accurate rubbing down between layers. The end result is a bit more hard wearing if it has been applied well.

15.7) Using Spirit Based Stain: Optional

Work outdoors, or in a well ventilated shed. Wear rubber gloves. It is messy stuff. Use small cotton rags to spread the stain.

Spirit-based wood dyes are commonly available at your builders' merchant. They are much easier to rub, apply evenly, and blend to the wood, than are water-based wood dyes. They are the best choice if you are going to finish with water-based lacquer. They are usually supplied in a variety of dark shades, in order to make less expensive light softwoods look like more expensive dark hardwoods. But they can be diluted with surgical spirit from your pharmacy store, to make them, of various lighter shades, more interesting to show the figuring of guitar woods. I recommend using spirit dyes which are diluted with surgical spirit: anything between 3:1 and 10:1 and 100:1.

Apply to scrap plywood and quickly lacquer a couple of coats to test the result.

15.8) Sunburst Staining: Exotic

Sunburst finishes are achieved by blending 2 or 3 shades of stain together. The sunburst could be on the front and back of the guitar. Few people ever look at the back of a guitar, so it is adequate to create a sunburst on the front, with simply the darker colour of it all over the back.

Use sprit-based stains for best soft blending. They can be re-rubbed with more spirit, and re-blended several times to get best results. The simplest way to create an attractive sunburst is to use just one spirit based stain. Dilute this 50:1 to make the soundboard front middle stain. Dilute this 7:1 to make the intermediary sunburst wash. Optionally put a trace of other colour dye into the intermediary sunburst wash.

Firstly apply the original stain over the back and sides and edges of the front. Then apply an intermediary wash on the outside of the front soundboard. Then apply the extremely diluted wash across the whole front soundboard. Blend all staining together with lots of rubbing of spirit lubricated cotton rags.

15.9) Bright Water-Based Dyes: Exotic

Water-based aniline dyes are the brightest, most colour-saturated that are generally available. They can be difficult to find in DIY shops. Search the Internet. I use Manns Classic Wood Dye which is available in red, blue, yellow, orange, brown, black. They are very bright colours. e.g. water-based red is fire-engine, whereas spirit-based red is burgundy. You can create any shade of any colour by mixing them in various proportions. e.g. simplest: blue + yellow = green. Mixing very small amounts of bright colours into bland colours, can be very effective at livening them up. The mix can work as an artist's palette.

Water-based dyes are difficult to blend in sunbursts. It is possible, with skill and a lot of rubbing, but tends to go blotchy. They are easiest to use for single colour guitars. Rub a lot, and use two coats, to get an even full colour.

You can finish with oil over water-based dye without problems.

It is possible to finish with water-based lacquer, if you use the following more complicated procedure. The problem you have to overcome, is that the lacquer will re-dissolve the dye, and redistribute it in a blotchy streaky manner, when you brush the lacquer. The perfect solution to the problem is to finish in 3 layers: dye; "paint"; lacquer. First dye the wood with two coats of dye. Second make a "paint" by mixing some of the lacquer with 25% of the same dye. Use this "paint" for the first two coats of lacquer. This will stabilise the colour thickly and evenly. Wash your brush immediately and thoroughly. Continue with several coats of clear lacquer.

However you intend to do your finishing procedure, practice on scrap wood before committing to your guitar.

15.10) Water-based Lacquer: Recommended

Modern water-based lacquer, or varnish, finishes have a very good set of characteristics: Good looking results; fairly hard-wearing; can be applied indoors; easy brush cleaning; environment friendly; satin or high-gloss finishing.

Polyurethane varnish was the first to be developed, and is OK and quite tough, but a bit soft for polishing well. Acrylic lacquer is better. The best lacquers are a bi-polymer mix of acrylic and polyurethane, or other polymers.

Avoid products that are called "satin varnish". They have extra unwanted chemicals in them to make the surface go satin when drying. Buy gloss lacquer or varnish. We will use a more sophisticated method of finishing to achieve a perfect satin finish.

A new, or perfectly cleaned, high quality brush is essential. 1 ½ inch wide with fine hair. Art shops have the best fine brushes at high prices. A top quality DIY shop brush should be adequate.

The best results are achieved with many thin coats of lacquer, rather than a few thick coats. Dip the brush in the lacquer only 3mm = 1/8 in each time. It is vitally important that you do not over-wet the surface and leave tear-drops behind, which will be very difficult to remove after they have dried. At the end of every coat application, look very carefully against the light, at every detail of every surface, and brush out any tear-drop. The purpose of all brushing is to create a strong flat multi-layer of lacquer of even thickness.

Day 1 (1 hour): Brush lacquer evenly with long smooth straight movements, all over the surface of the front and sides of the body, and over the neck plate area of the back. Do the same on the back cover. Allow to soak in and dry for a half hour. Brush over the whole surface for a second coat of lacquer. Dry for a day. Total 2 coats lacquer.

Day 2 (4 hours): Rub down quickly and gently with an abralon P600 abrasive pad to remove grain swell roughness. Be very gentle on edges and corners. Then apply another four coats of lacquer at one hour intervals. Brush evenly, with long smooth straight movements. Alternate the direction of the brushing by 90 deg between each coat, so as to make the most flat end result. Total 6 coats lacquer.

Day 3 (4 hours): Rub down and apply another 4 coats of lacquer as on day 2. Total 10 coats lacquer.

Day 4 Optional (4 hours): If you have used dark stains, then apply another 4 coats of lacquer as on day 2. Total 14 coats lacquer. Accidentally rubbing through dark stains at a late stage would be a major set-back.

Day 5 Optional (4 hours): If you will be going on to finish this with a high gloss, then apply another 4 coats of lacquer as on day 2. Total 18 coats lacquer. Accidentally rubbing through polished lacquer at a late stage would be a major set-back.

Between these 3 to 5 days of brushing lacquer, or a few more, do not leave much more than 2 days between any two coats. Chemical reactions are involved, in which each coat needs to polymerise perfectly clearly with the next coat. If you wait too long, the next layer does not blend clearly with the previous layer, and faint ghost lines appear in the lacquer.

15.11) Satin Finish

Hang up the guitar body, and leave it, for as long as possible, for the lacquer to harden. Wait 4 days or more. The lacquer will harden faster if kept warm, and harden slower if kept cold.

Firstly, flatten the lacquer perfectly to remove all brush marks. Use P 600 sandpaper dry on a sanding block for the flat front and back. Use a flexible P600 abralon pad dry for the sides and edges and corners. Go very gently on edges and corners, it is all too easy to rub through to expose raw wood. Frequently brush off the dust of the surface of the guitar, and view it all carefully against the light. Make sure that all hills are removed, and that the flat surface goes just down to eradicate all valleys, and no further.

Pay attention to all my advice on sanding. Polishing is fundamentally the same process, and set of issues as sanding, but all done on a much smaller microscopic scale of sizes. When polishing, it is more important than ever to keep your abrasives and polishes and cloths perfectly clean. If your polishing pad or cloth gets contaminated with rougher tiny grit, it can rub in deeper scratches that will never get removed with later finer polishing.

Finish as satin, by rubbingP1000 abralon on all lacquered surfaces. Always work in one straight direction. Firstly, rub around all the curved sides of the guitar, completing a circuit of the perimeter. Secondly, rub the front and the back of the guitar. Rub everywhere in the same straight direction from rump to neck.

If you fancy a finer more shiny satin finish, then go further onto rub in the same style with dry P2000 abralon. Not everything about the finer shine is better. It shows sticky finger marks, and wear marks, sooner.

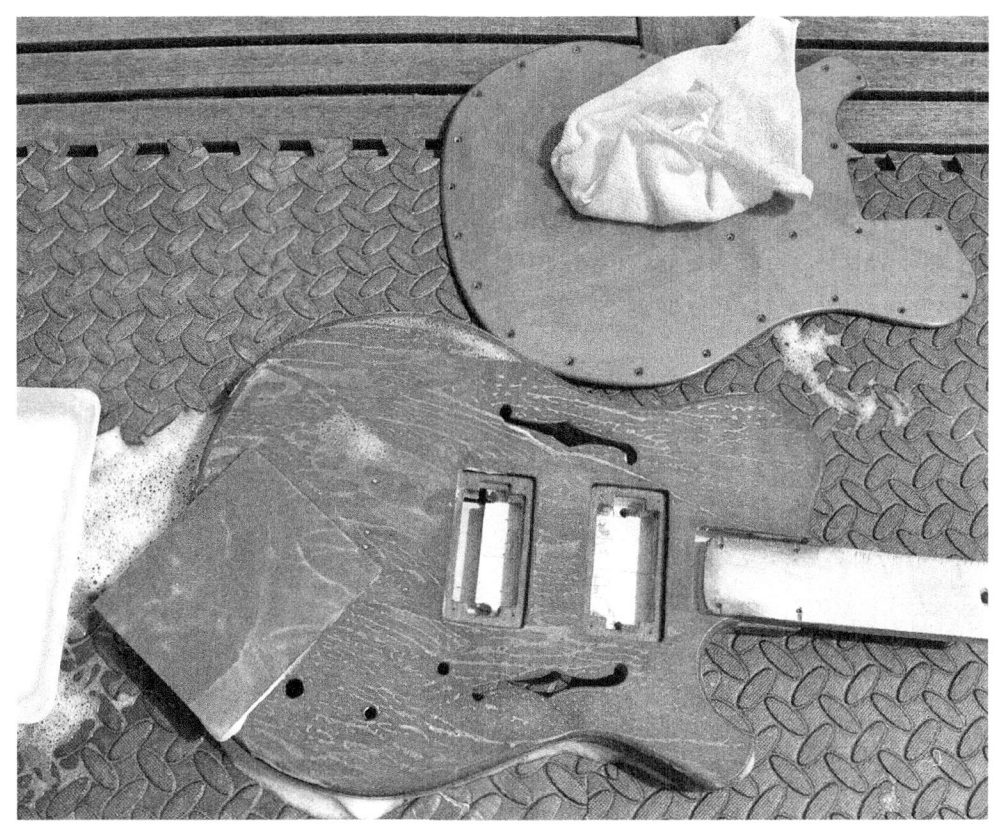

15.12) High Gloss Finish: Optional

Make sure that you have already created a perfect P2000 satin finish, before you go on to polish it into a high-gloss finish. The high gloss finish will highlight any unwanted valleys in the lacquer.

Firstly wait 6 days or more after the satin finish. Hang up the guitar body in a warm place, and leave it for as long as possible for the lacquer to further harden. Hard lacquer will polish much better than soft lacquer. The longer you wait, the better the end result will be.

Polishing is then a process of going through several stages of finer microscopic gentle abrasion, to flatten the surface of the lacquer to an optical quality. Fine abrasives, then lubricated super-fine abrasives, then liquid polishes which contain super-super fine abrasives.

Abralon abrasives can be lubricated with soapy water, in order to reduce the risk of larger pieces of grit causing scratches.

Rub straight, a lot, using a wet P2000 abralon pad. Dry and clean with a cotton cloth. View carefully against the light. Redo until you see perfection of an even appearance everywhere.

Repeat the same process again, this time use a wet P4000 abralon pad. At the end of this, the guitar should look like it has a vintage slightly-dull gloss finish, with no scratches. It will need further application of polishes on cloths to get to a mirror finish.

The right type of polishes to use, are those that are finely to finely-finely lubricated abrasives, intended to be used on a cotton cloth, hand pad, or motorised buffing pad. They are most frequently purposed for polishing car repair re-paints. Unfortunately, they do not seem to have a standardised way of measuring how fine or fine-fine their abrasion is. I use Fareclar G3 Regular Compound to get a gloss finish, followed by Fareclar G10 Finishing Compound to get a high-gloss finish.

Do not use anything called furniture polish. It is just soft wax or similar, which simply fills in the microscopic scratches and roughness with a temporary fill-in. It will look good for only a few weeks until it dries or rubs out. Stuff sold as "guitar polish" is much the same as furniture polish. It can be used months and years later, to beautify a used guitar body, but is not the right stuff to use during the making of a new guitar.

Make a handy polishing pad by folding up some cotton cloth. Apply some regular polish to it. Rub extensively in straight lines. Clean off with a slightly wet clean cotton cloth. View carefully against the light. Repeat until perfectly gloss everywhere.

Repeat the same process again, using finishing polish, to achieve a high-gloss finish. When it looks perfectly mirror-like, it's time to pop the Champagne!

15.13) Spray Painting

A quick, slightly dangerous, and very messy, way to finish a guitar is to use aerosol spray paint. It is widely available at car part stores. I do not recommend it. As well as being messy, it requires considerable skill to get a good result. Work outdoors on a dry calm day, with the little wind behind you. Always wear a mask and safety goggles. Consider carefully what else you will end up unintentionally painting with the over-spray! There will be a lot of over-spray when painting a guitar. This can be a serious problem.

Apply two or three thin coats of primer at one hour intervals. Spray with a series of strokes from off one side of the guitar, across the surface of the guitar, finishing off the guitar. This is to avoid the spluttering, when the spray starts and stops, spoiling the surface of the paint. Do not spray too much in any one coat. You will get nasty tear-drops as the paint runs before it dries.

Leave the primer paint to dry and harden for a day. Inspect the results carefully against the light. If you do get any tear-drops, then scrape them off using a razor blade. Do not scrape too far. Rub down with P600 abralon to get a perfect even surface. If it has any defects, then do another day of spraying primer paint, then the next day rub down again with P600 abralon.

Spray four to eight thin coats of colour paint. Make sure it dries well and hard between each coat. This might take one or two days.

If you are using metallic colour paint, you should finish off with two coats of compatible car lacquer paint.

The simple spray-paint finish might be good enough for you. Just buff it up a bit with a microfibre cloth. If you want perfection, then wait a week for the paint to harden, then polish it to high-gloss using the process described above in 15.12).

16) Fitting Pickups

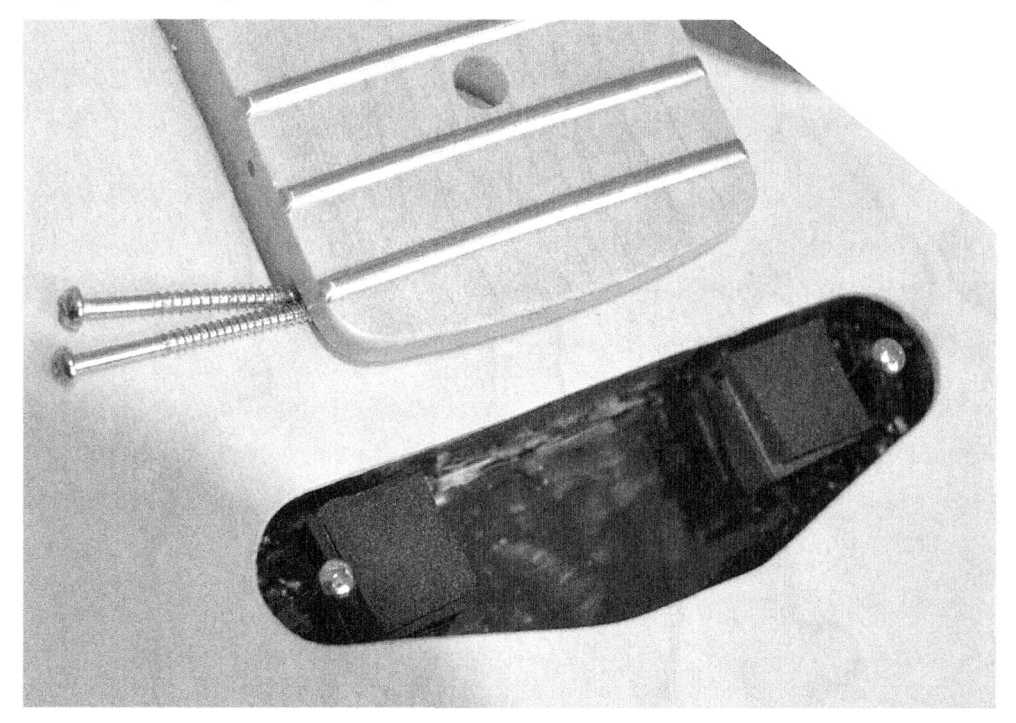

A Fender Stratocaster has it's pickups fixed onto the plastic scratchplate, with screws from the front of the scratchplate, screwing into the black fibre back-plate of the pickup. The pickups have no connection to the deeper body wood.

A Rees guitar has the pickups fixed to the deep body wood of the centre spine. The front soundboard does not touch the pickups at all. This is much the same construction method as the neck pickup of the original vintage Fender Telecaster.

Here is a photo of the pickup cavity, being fitted with height-adjustment screws and foam pads, before the pickup is to be fitted. The bottom surface is laminate C, covered in optional sticky-back copper foil for hum rejection, and roughly painted black for optional cosmetic detail. The two height-adjustment screws are of the type most frequently used to mount Fender bass pickups. They are 2.5mm = 3/32in thick, and 32mm = 1 1/4in long. The two dark grey foam pads press the pickup up against the two height-adjustment screws. Those two screws hold the pickup down towards the deep wood of the central spine of the guitar. The pads are fixed on with double-sided-sticky-tape. When the pickup is fitted, that will further clamp all the foam together forever.

It is very important to fix the two height-adjustment screws in the right position, and exactly vertical to the front. They need to be nicely fixed, and free running, screwing up and down. Take the plastic cover off one of your pickups, place it exactly in the middle of the pickup cavity of the guitar body. Mark the location of the two screws with a pencil. Drill the two height-adjustment screw holes 2mm = 5/64in straight through from the front to the back. (The back cover will hide this later.)

Try out the free running of the holes, with height-adjustment screws, lubricated with any oil or grease. Even a small spot of margarine or butter will do. They must be able to be adjusted, up and down, reliably and smoothly, with gentle force.

Screw in the height-adjustment screws completely so that they poke out the back. See where the bridge pickup screws might interfere with the bridge mechanism. Trim off a bit on the side of the bridge tongue if necessary, to avoid any unwanted contact of the screw with the tongue.

Getting the foam pads right is an art, both because the availability of foams is so variable, and because various pickups have slightly different depths. The stiffness of the foam wants to be fairly firm, so as to hold the weight of the pickup. The stiffness also needs to be soft enough, so that you can fairly easily squash it to 1/3 thickness between your finger and thumb. The original thickness needs to be such that it could hold the pickup, up against the guitar strings, with a gentle pressure. You might use 2 or 3 layers of foams to get exactly the right foam pad height.

Try out a pair of foam pads on one pickup first. Start with a foam pad thickness of 16mm = 5/8in. If your foam is very stiff you might want the pad a bit thinner. If your foam is soft, you might want the pad a bit thicker.

Unscrew and remove the height-adjustment screws. Keep the two foam pads lightly fixed in place. Place the pickup with it's cover onto the foam pads. Take great care not to damage the very fine wires of the pickup, which are exposed around the perimeter of the pickup, and near the middle of the fibre back-plate of the pickup. Push the two height-adjustment screws through the pickup cover and the screw holes of the pickup fibre back-plate. Screw them down into the two lubricated holes of the deep wood.

Check that the pickups can be easily adjusted over a wide range of pickup height. Highest such that the tops of the bridge poles are 12mm = ½ in above the soundboard. Lowest being screwed down to 3mm = 1/8in above the level of the soundboard. Make sure that the sides of the pickups never touch the soundboard.

17) Controls and Wiring

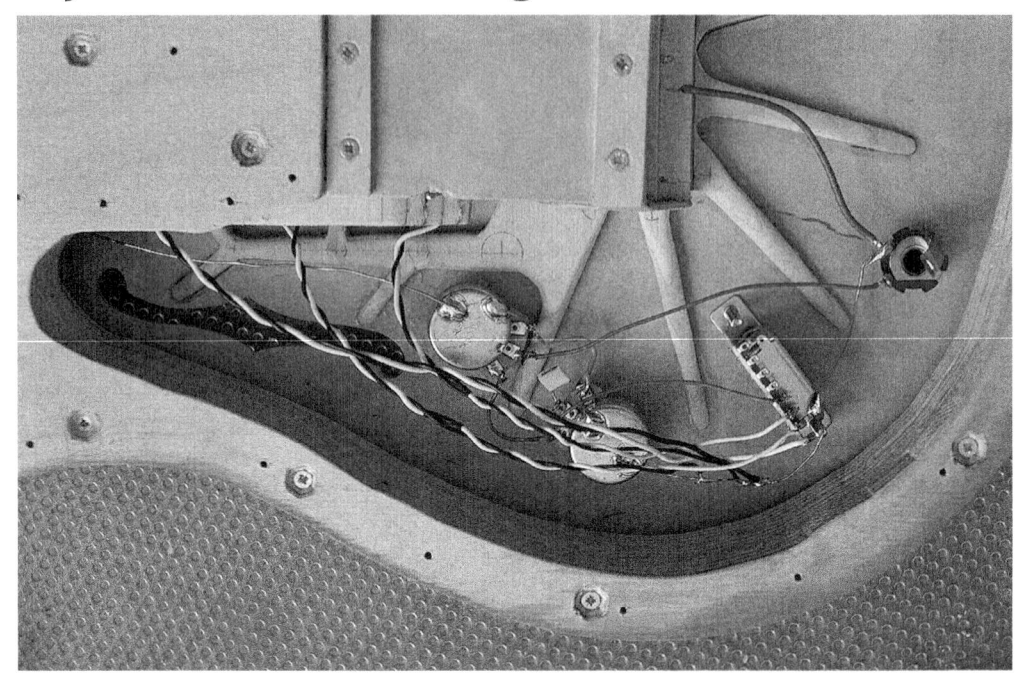

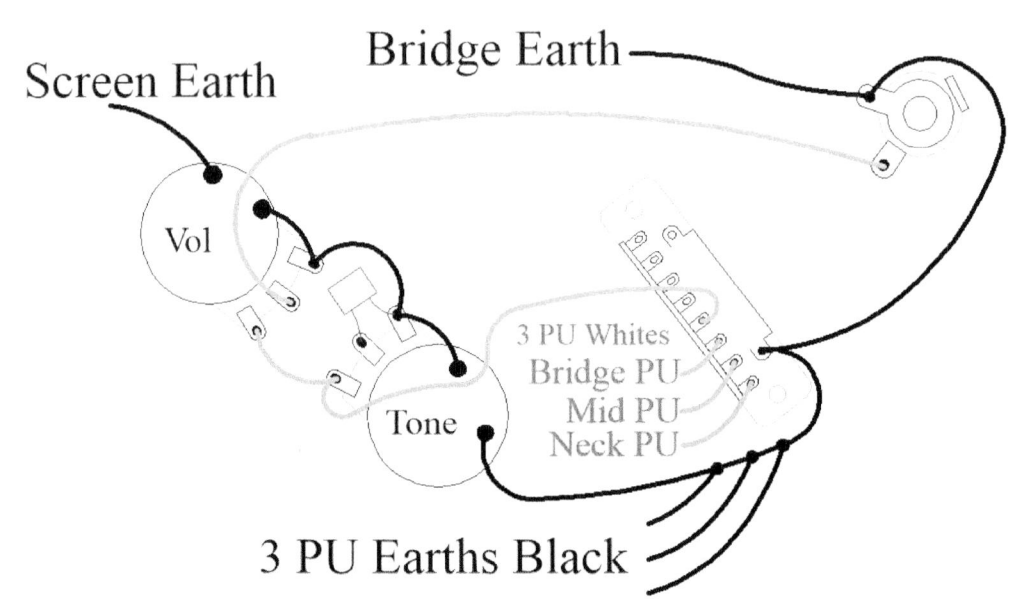

Bridge Earth

Screen Earth

Vol

3 PU Whites
Bridge PU
Mid PU
Tone
Neck PU

3 PU Earths Black

Here is a photo of the electric controls, and a wiring diagram. The earth wires are shown in black, and the signal wires are shown in pink or light grey.

17.1) Soldering

You will need to use solder to make all the wiring joints. Use thin solder wire. At the time of writing, there are two types of solder in common use world-wide for guitar wiring. They have opposite hazards and ease of use.

Traditional lead solder is made as an alloy of half tin with half lead. This alloy was chosen as having the lowest melting point, and best sticking properties. However, anything containing lead is nowadays discouraged, because lead is a slowly cumulative poison. Solder containing lead may be banned in some countries. It is widely available on Ebay. If you handle lead solder, either wear rubber gloves, or wash your hands immediately afterwards. Wear a face mask, and avoid inhaling fumes from the soldering process. Lead solder is easy to use with any low-cost amateur soldering iron, and sticks well to all component surfaces.

Modern Lead-Free Solder is made of tin, with just a trace of copper added. To be able to stick solder to the larger surfaces of components, it needs to be applied with a professional soldering iron: high-power 45W or 60W; temperature controlled at about 380 or 400 degC. It is still considerably more difficult to work with, and to get components to stick together reliably. It avoids most of the health hazards, having no lead. However you should still avoid inhaling the fumes from the flux in the solder wire. Lead-free solder is stronger than lead solder if it is applied perfectly.

17.2) Potentiometers
These pots must both be type A = logarithmic = audio.
They should not be the other type B = linear.
They should be of resistance 250kOhm.
Pots having one inch diameter are more reliable and hard-wearing than smaller, cheaper micro-pots. I use Alfa pots.
The control knobs can be any lightweight plastic.

17.3) Tone Control and Capacitor
I choose 33nF plastic capacitors for stability, and best mid-tone to my ears. If you want a warmer mid-tone then use 47nF. If you want a brighter mid-tone then use 22nF capacitors.

(Over the Internet, there are a lot of "snake-oil" stories about tone capacitors. Most stories originate because expensive, very low leakage capacitors, are very desireable in valve amplifiers. In amps there are huge dangerous DC voltage differences, between the output of one valve, and the input of the next valve. Each pair of valves in the chain are joined together by these expensive capacitors. Any very, very small, leakage current through the coupling capacitor, which joins one valve to the next, can upset the input bias of the next valve. If the input bias is slightly wrong, then that valve will sound not so good. The performance of each valve is dependant upon the quality of the coupling capacitor that feeds it's signal.

There are no significant DC voltage differences in the electronics of a guitar. In a guitar, a capacitor is a capacitor, the tone being affected just by the nF value of the capacitor.)

My circuit for the tone pot and capacitor is my invention. It is not exactly the same as factory guitars. It provides a more progressive control of tone, from one end to the other, of the tone control. You must use Log=A= Audio type pots for this to work at it's best.

17.4) 5-Way Switch
The 5-way switch needs to be light-weight. I choose an Alfa switch.

17.5) The Earth Wiring
All earth wires are shown black on the diagram. Earth wiring provides the return path for all important electric signals, which are very tiny electronic currents from all pickups and components. You can most easily use any solid bare tinned copper wire for most earth wiring. 22SWG is very good. Multi-strand insulated wire is also good, green colour shows the earth intension.

Earth wiring also provides silence and immunity from unwanted airborne external Electro-Magnetic interference. EM interference adds unwanted buzzes, crackles, and pops to the electric sound. EM interference comes, through the air, like radio waves, from computers, mobile phones, fluorescent lighting, air-conditioning units, motor vehicles, electric motors, guitar valve amp transformers, etc., etc.

The guitar bridge must be earthed. There must be a multi-strand earth wire, bared for a final half inch, splayed out and trapped to provide wide contact under the metal bridge. The wire passes through the wood of the bridge block to the inside of the guitar. This absorbs all the EM interference which is picked up by the guitarist's body, and connected to the guitar strings.

Pickups collect EM interference. In order to minimise the EM interference to the pickups, fix a shielding layer of sticky-back copper foil onto the inside spine of laminate C. That will isolate the pickups from the main wood of the body, which collects EM interference from the body of the guitarist. Press it down firmly. Solder an earth wire to the copper foil, and solder the other end of the wire to an earthed component.

Solder all the earth wires, show in black on the diagram. Some of the earth wires are soldered onto the back of the can of a pot, and the frame of the switch

17.6) The Signal Wiring

Signal wiring provides selection of pickups, volume and tone adjustments, and output to the jack socket. Each of the white wires of pickups goes to the switch which selects one or two of them. The output from the switch goes to the tone and vol pots. The tone control works by adding a variable amount of the tone capacitor, attenuating higher frequencies. The variable output from the vol pot goes to the output jack socket.

Solder the tone capacitor onto two of the tags of the tone pot. Solder all signal wires using insulated multi-strand wire. Keep them fairly short, and positioned so that they do not rattle on the soundboard.

17.7) Touch Testing the Wiring

Make sure to use a reliable amp that is plugged into a good mains socket with reliable earth. If an amp is not reliably earthed, then it is not safe to use with any guitar. All electric guitars and amps connect the guitarist to the earth system via the strings of the guitar. Plug the guitar body into the amp, with a normal guitar to amp coax cable. Place the guitar body on a table on it's front, with the back cover removed, so you can touch all of it's inside components.

Touch the signal tag of the jack socket with your finger and it should buzz. The EM interference from your body is going into the input of the amp. If it does not buzz, then the guitar is not connected to a working amp.

Touch the earth tag of the jack socket and it should not buzz. The EM interference from your finger is going silently straight to earth, and not into the input of the amp.

Touch all the parts that are earthed. None of them should buzz. If any do, then you have an earth wire missing or a bad solder joint. The point in the circuit where buzzing meets non-buzzing is where the problem is.

Touch all the parts that are in-circuit, and they should buzz as expected when selected. Each of the controls will influence this. Start with vol full-on; tone full-on; middle pickup selected.

17.8) Tap Testing Pickups and Controls

This is the easiest way to verify that all the pickups are working, and that their selections are correct. This can be a very useful test of any old finished guitar, without having to undo the back, nor alter nor undo anything. You might like to firstly do this test on any known good guitar, so that you know what to expect when you test your new guitar.

Place the guitar flat on it's back on a table, and plug it into an amp. During each of several tests, gently tap any pole, of each of the three pickups, with a steel screw-driver. When a pickup is working and selected, you should hear a solid bright clunk through the amp. When a pickup is not selected, you should hear nothing from the amp.

Start with the controls Vol full-on and Tone full-on, and the pickup selector at the middle position. Tap the middle pickup poles with your screwdriver. You should hear a solid bright clunk. Tap each of the other pickups and you should hear nothing from the amp.

When you turn the volume control, you should hear a variably quieter clunk. When you turn the tone control, you should hear a variably duller less-bright clunk.

Test the effect of the 5-way pickup selector for each of it's 5 positions. During each of the 5 tests, tap all 3 of the pickups, to verify that their engagement is:
pos 1) bridge pu
pos 2) bridge pu + mid pu
pos 3) mid pu
pos 4) mid pu + neck pu
pos 5) neck pu

17.9) Optional Testing with a Multi-Meter

Using an electronic multi-meter is not necessary for this project, but can sometimes be useful, if you have one. It is particularly useful to test a doubtful individual pickup, by itself. If the very fine winding wire of a pickup gets broken, then the resistance will be infinity, and not registered on the meter. If, much more unusually, a winding has got shortened to earth, then the resistance will be measured at zero.

You can test the resistance of pickups on any completed guitar, by testing the resistance at the two contacts of the jack socket. You might solder two insulated wires onto a spare jack-plug, than can be plugged into any of your guitars, and connected to your multi-meter.

Make sure that the volume control is completely full-on. Any back-off of the volume control will add a lot of resistance to the measurement. A high-quality S-type pickup has a resistance of about 6.4kOhm, maybe as low as 5kOhm, and possibly as high as 16kOhm. Different pickup designs have different resistances.

When two pickups are in-circuit, as at 5-way switch positions 2 and 4, the resistance, measured at the jack socket, should be half of one pickup, so maybe 3.2kOhm

18) The Neck

18.1) Choosing a Compatible Neck

The neck can be any S-Type neck, such that might fit on a Fender Stratocaster.

The neck heel has a width of 2 3/16 in = 55.6mm

The scale length, nut to bridge is 25 ½ in = 648mm
The distance between the edge of the nut nearest the frets, and the 12th fret should be exactly half that. 12 ¾ in = 324mm

The distance from the Y0 end of the neck pocket, to the frets should be:
fret 22 at 2mm = 5/64 in
fret 21 at 13mm = ½ in

18.2) Make the Neck Shim

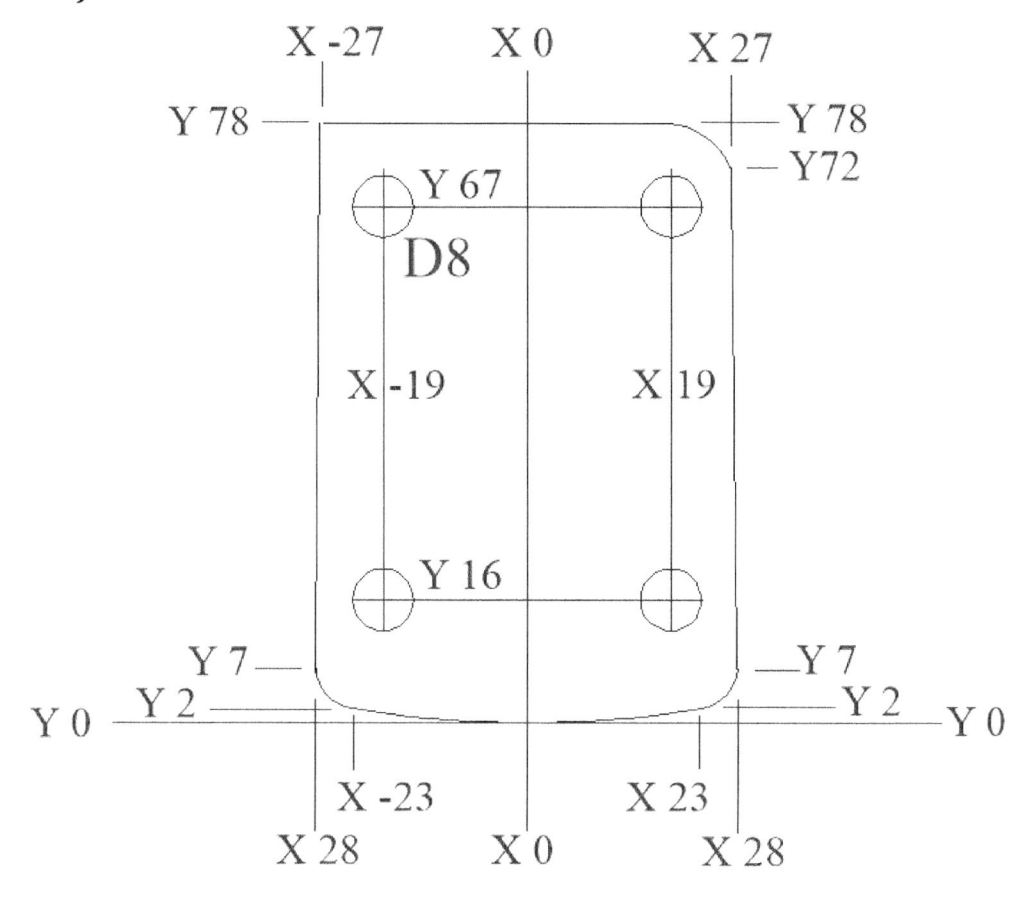

```
        X -27      X 0      X 27
  Y 78 ──┬─────────────────┬── Y 78
                              ── Y72
           ⊕ Y 67      ⊕
              D8
           X -19      X 19

           ⊕ Y 16      ⊕

       Y 7 ──┐              ┌── Y 7
  Y 0 ── Y 2 ─┴────────────┴── Y 2 ── Y 0
              X -23    X 23
          X 28    X 0    X 28
```

The neck shim is made of 3mm or 1/8 in plywood. It fixes the neck at the right height relative to the bridge height.

18.3) Dressing Frets

Low cost guitar necks most often have rough, and even sharp, ends to the frets. Expensive guitars have the ends of the frets dressed to perfection, such that they are all nicely rounded, polished and smooth to touch. Guitarists talk about the quality, and nice played-in feel, of vintage guitar necks. They are often talking about some many years of playing, resulting in gentle abrasion and polishing of the fret ends.

P600 abralon is a quick, very efficient, way to sort this out on a low-cost neck. Rub extensively, smoothly rounding at 45 deg over the length of the neck, over both ends of the frets. The soft abralon pad rounds off the ends of the frets.

Repeat with P1000 then P2000 then P4000 abralon for polished results.

18.4) Finishing the Wood of the Neck

If your neck is gloss lacquered, it might be slightly sticky in playing feel. Particularly so, if it is a used neck, that has got a bit dirty. You can greatly improve the playing feel of the back of any guitar neck, by rubbing it clean, and change it from sticky gloss, to smooth fast satin finish. Use a P2000 abralon pad, and rub it just enough to create a satin finish, and no more. Rub up and down along the length of the neck.

If your neck is a new bare wood neck, then you need to finish it with lacquer. Refer to my previous chapter on finishing. If you have a dark wood fingerboard, then you will want to mask it off with masking tape, so that it does not receive any lacquer.

18.5) Fitting a Nut

It is easiest to use a neck that has a nut already fitted. Bone nuts might be very slightly best for tone. Plastic nuts are also very good. The right shape, positions, and heights, of the string grooves, are the most important qualities. It is most important to get the string heights within the nut slots perfect, for every string to be easily played. Adjusting the depth of the nut slot grooves for all strings, is absolutely critical to the performance of any guitar. See chapter 20)

At this stage, it is best to shape the nut, and fit it dry in it's slot, with no glue. Wait until the final setup stage before glueing the nut.

18.6) Fitting Tuners

The design and manufacturing quality of tuners has evolved, and improved considerably over the past 70 years. They have been developed from poor-performance-expensive, to high-performance-moderate-cost. Modern necks and tuners have 10mm = 13/32in location holes in the headstock.

Vintage tuners used smaller holes, and new reproductions of them are available. My advice is to avoid them, because they wear-out quickly, and then become inaccurate.

The best stability, easiest to use, modern tuners, are of the locking tuner type. Each tuner has a 10mm nut to fix it tightly on the headstock. It also has either a small screw, or a pin, at the back, to stop it from rotating. The easiest to fit by hand, are those with a small screw. Pins need super-accurate location holes, created by CAM machinery.

Put the tuners on the headstock, and do up the 10mm nuts by hand only. Rotate the tuners to ensure that all the tuner buttons are in line. Drill 1.5mm = 1/16in holes for the small screws. Fix the small screws. Use a box spanner to tighten up the 10mm nuts firmly.

18.7) Adjusting the Neck Truss-rod

Guitars need necks that are straight, in order to play well with gentle fingering of the strings onto the frets. For perfection, the neck should be just very slightly bowed forward when under string tension, so that in the middle there is a tiny bit more room for the strings to vibrate. "Tiny" is rather dependent on playing style. However, if you simply start with a neck that is perfectly straight before you put it on the guitar, then the string tension will bend it just slightly forward, which is probably close to your perfect set-up.

The steel truss rod is built into the wood of the neck, such that it holds the neck straight against the strong bending force of the guitar strings. At one end or the other of the neck, there is an adjustment nut. Most adjustment nuts use Allen keys to adjust the truss rod.

Some necks have a screw-driver adjustment at the heel of the neck. These can only be adjusted with the neck removed from the body.

When you screw this nut clockwise tighter, it will bend the neck back, and lower the string action. When you screw this nut anti-clockwise looser, the neck will relax and bend forwards, and make the string action higher. The adjustment nut should be a bit stiff, but easy to adjust without huge force. If it is fully undone it goes loose. If it is badly over-tightened it will probably jam.

If you are getting the neck from a donor guitar, check that the neck is straight before you dismantle it. Necks tend to relax and bend forwards with age, making the string action higher, and more difficult to play. Necks should be checked, and if necessary tightened, every few years.

If you need to tighten the truss rod on a working guitar, first slacken the strings a bit. Then tighten the truss rod, then bring the strings back to pitch. Waggle the neck around a bit to spread the stresses between truss rod and wood, evenly along the length of the neck. Re-tune.

There are several ways to test the straightness of a neck:

Test Neck Straightness by Feel

Here is a great trick: powerful; requires no tools at all; and which surprisingly few people know about! For a working guitar, tune it to pitch. Place the guitar flat on it's back on a table. On any string, press the string down on the first fret, and down on any high fret. The string itself is then positioned fully down, and is perfectly straight due to the string tension. Observe that in the middle, the string should be just about not touching the frets, with a very small gap. To do a complete survey of neck straightness, and fret heights, repeat this procedure on all strings, and over various small to large spans of the frets. This can give you a full understanding of which parts of the neck and frets are inaccurate. Over smaller spans you can test it quickly, and very sensitively, by pressing the string down across any span between your two little fingers, and feeling it in the mid parts with your two thumbs or index fingers.

Test Neck Straightness by Sight

The straightness of any neck, on or off the guitar, can be seen fairly critically by sight. View closely with one eye, from one end of the neck, looking at all the frets in a line from your eye to the distance. This is also a good way to see if any fret is high.

Test Neck Straightness by Measurement

Hold a two foot ruler or straight-edge against the fretboard. Rock it side to side to feel for a gap or hump. View closely from the side.

On a neck that is off the guitar, slide a flat wood block up and down the fretboard to detect any high frets.

Adjusting a New Neck

If you are starting with a new neck, the truss rod will usually be not tensioned Tightening the truss rod will bring it straight. Over-tightening the truss rod will bend the neck back. Tighten it bit by bit, and check the straightness each time.

Put a moderate bending stress on the neck with your hands, wobbling forwards and backwards, in order to get the truss rod to stretch out evenly within it's slot in the neck.

19) Final Assembly

19.1) Strap Buttons

Screw two strap buttons onto the body, into 2mm = 5/64in holes.

Big buttons provide more security for the strap, to avoid any risk of dropping the guitar during excited moments of music performance. The neck end button might be angled back a bit towards the neck, so that the strap is more reliably anchored.

19.2) Bridge

Screw the bridge tightly onto the front soundboard with the 5 suitable chrome-plated screws, into the 2mm = 5/64in holes. Hidden between the back of the metal bridge, and the front of the soundboard, should be the trapped splayed-out strands of the bridge earth wire.

19.3) Screwing the Neck On

The neck is attached with four 45mm = 1 3/4in neck screws. Do not use screws that are at all shorter than that. The screws go in from the back through the metal neck plate, then the body, then neck pocket shim, then into the neck heel. The drill holes in the neck heel should be 3mm = 1/8in.

Firstly screw in the four neck screws lightly. Check that the neck is perfectly straight in line with the bridge, by viewing it with one eye from the headstock down to the bridge. We will fully tighten the neck screws, later in the set-up, after the strings are put on the guitar.

20) Final Set-up

20.1) Put the Strings On

Use nickel wound steel electric guitar strings. I favour a string set of size 11 to 49 on these semi-acoustics, which feels about the same as a set of 10 to 46 on a solid-body guitar. Feed each string through it's anchor hole, at the tail end of the metal bridge, and up through the middle of it's bridge-piece. A useful trick, to get the string to go up and exit over the bridge-piece is this: Press the string down towards the body at the outside of the anchor hole, which then waggles the inside part of the string up as it proceeds through the bridge-piece. Each string then continues up the neck, over the nut, and under any string-tree, and then fixed into it's tuner. Tighten up the strings to a rough pitch of tune.

20.2) Set the Neck Tightly

The tension of the strings will pull the neck firmly into the neck pocket with long-term stability. Look at the strings above the high frets of the finger-board. They should be in the middle of the finger-board when the neck is straight in-line. If the neck is rotated a tiny bit either way, the strings will be set a bit to one side of the finger-board. If so, pull the neck to one side to rotate it into perfect alignment, with the strings in the middle of the fret-board, and tighten up all four neck screws.

20.3) Bridge Height

Each bridge-piece has a pair of small screws which wind it up and down using a small Allen key. Wind both the screws exactly together, going up or down, so that the bridge piece is always flat in parallel with the body. This provides best stability for every bridge-piece, each supported by their two screws. This enables you to set the action height of the strings over the fretboard.

Bridge Height by Measurement

I set up electric guitars with the following string heights above the 12th fret. Each measurement is from the top of the fret to the bottom of the guitar string.

E 2.0mm   bass
A 1.8mm

D 1.6mm
G 1.4mm
B 1.3mm
E 1.2mm   treble

You might like them a bit higher if you are a rough player, or a tiny bit lower if you are a gentle player. If they are too high, the guitar becomes difficult to play, and hurts your fingers. If they are too low, the strings will rattle and buzz on the frets.

Bridge Height by Feel

You can further adjust all of these string heights to your personal perfection. This is done by playing feel, not measurement. Firstly do an overall measurement setup, then play the guitar a lot, over a couple of days. At every stage, do many playing tests over all the frets. For each string: wind the bridge-piece down until the playing just starts to get buzzes and rattles on the frets. Then wind it back up, just enough to no longer get any trouble, with your personal variety of playing styles.

20.4) Neck Pocket Shim

If the action needs to be made a lot higher or lower, sanding a removable shim is an easy way to make the adjustment up or down. It will tip the angle of the neck forward or back slightly. Usually this is not needed nor wanted. Make sure that the neck is properly straight, before you start attacking the neck shim.

If you have to sand the shim, place a sheet of sandpaper on a flat surface. Rub the shim flat on that, while putting most pressure towards one end of the shim. Small differences make large differences to the string action height. The result is a shim that is very slightly wedge shaped. Do this on only one side of the shim. Make sure that the new sanded surface is exactly flat by holding a ruler over the surface.

Try gently screwing the neck and shim onto the body, fit one middle string, and test the action height. Repeat the procedure until it is correct.

20.5) Bridge Intonation by Measurement

Tune the guitar to concert pitch before you start. Put a drop of oil on each string, where it hangs off the bridge, to lubricate the movement of the bridge pieces underneath the strings.

Intonation is the art of getting each string to vibrate at exactly the right frequency note, on every fret. It is controlled and set up by the forward and back adjustment of each of the six bridge pieces. The 12th fret should be exactly twice the frequency of the open string, creating a note an octave above the open string. Simple theory says that the 12th fret should be exactly half-way between the nut and the bridge. In reality, that is not exactly so. This is because real strings each have a different stiffness, which produces a different small end-effect at the bridge.

For best intonation, each bridge-piece is adjusted back a very small number of mm, to make the string slightly longer than theory. This compensates for the string stiffness end-effect, and brings each string into correct intonation.

Different string stiffness needs different end-effect compensation. The stiffer the string, the further back the bridge piece should be, wound to lengthen the string. So overall, the bass strings are longer than treble strings, and have their bridge pieces further back. However, the stiffness of a string is mostly determined by the thickness of it's core. The extra winding on the bass strings does not add a lot to the stiffness. For a normal electric string set, having three wound strings, the pattern of bridge pieces will be like the following diagram:

Average Intonation Line

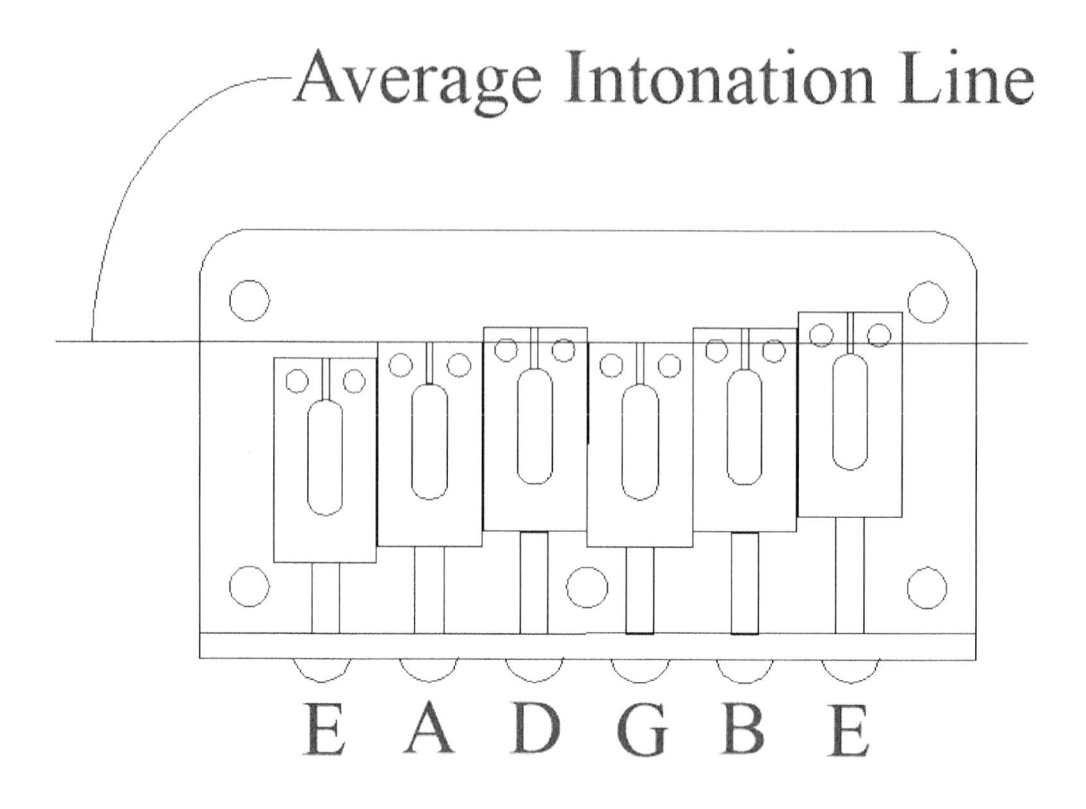

E A D G B E

In order to simplify the measurements and adjustments of all of this, it is helpful to introduce the concept of a single Average Intonation Line (AIL).

The correct AIL gets the average of the vibrating string lengths correct. This is the most important set-up parameter for intonation. Following that, the small incremental measurements of individual bridge pieces, are easy to add in reliably, as a minor adjustment.

For a normal set of nickel wound steel electric strings, the front edge of the bridge pieces will be approximately at:

E: AIL + 1.5mm
A: AIL
D: AIL – 1.5mm
G: AIL
B: AIL – 1.5mm
E: AIL – 3mm

But where is the AIL? - It depends slightly on the weight of the string set. Heavy strings have greater stiffness, and so they need the bridge pieces to be moved back a bit, to lengthen the strings and provide more compensation.

String Length (often called "scale length") is the length of the string that is vibrating. It is measured from the front edge of the nut, closest to the vibrating string, to the front edge of the bridge piece, closest to the vibrating string. For a standard 25 ½ inch scale length neck, the theoretical string length would be 25.5 in = 648mm.

However, real-world AILs, with compensation for various string sets, have the following vibrating string lengths, and Ycoords relative to the neck pocket of the body:
Nickel wound steel string sets:
10-46 String Set: AIL 649mm; Y-181
11-49 String Set: AIL 650mm; Y-182
12-54 String Set: AIL 651mm; Y-183

The front edge of the nut, nearest to the vibrating strings, is at Y coord 468mm.

20.6) Bridge Intonation by Tuner

Setting the intonation by measuring with a good tuner is the most accurate method. Do the following for each string: Measure the open string frequency and tune it to pitch. Measure the note when playing the 12th fret. It should be the same note as the open string, but an octave higher. It is exactly twice the frequency of the open string. If the 12th fret is a bit sharp (higher freq), then wind the bridge piece back a bit to lengthen the string. If the 12th fret is a bit flat (lower freq), then wind the bridge piece forward a bit to shorten the string. Tune and repeat until perfect.

20.7) Bridge Intonation by Ear

If you have good pitch hearing, you can set the intonation by ear. You do not need a tuner. Use the same procedure as when using a tuner. You might find it easier to compare the 12th fret with the first harmonic of the open string. That should be the same note and same frequency as the 12th fret when the intonation is correct. Play the first harmonic by touching the string very lightly with a left finger above the 12th fret, and pluck the string between the pickups.

20.8) Pickup Heights

Each of the 3 pickups has a height adjustment screw at the treble end, and one at the bass end. Adjusting these 6 screws, sets up the pickups, to provide the best set of voices for your playing style. Screwing clockwise brings a pickup closer to the strings and makes it louder.

For an exciting rock tone, with great dynamic range from gentle to rough playing, the pickups each want to be close to the strings. However, they must never touch the strings, even when you are playing on the high frets and playing aggressively. If any strongly vibrating string touches a pickup, it sounds awful, with a nasty discordant buzz and rattle.

There are other considerations. If you want a smoother jazzy tone, unscrew the pickups down a bit, maybe 3 mm = 1/8in further away from the strings. If you want a pickup to feel a bit brighter, set the treble end of the pickup close to the strings, and the bass end of the pickup further away from the strings. If you want a pickup to feel a bit warmer with stronger bass, do the opposite.

Most guitarists like all three pickups to sound out at the same loudness. Play with switching between pickup switch positions 1 and 3 and 5, to compare the loudness of the 3 pickups. If a pickup is extra loud, then wind it down a bit, further away from the strings.

20.9) Pickup Poles

S-Type pickup poles are not individually adjustable. Of course, you can alter the overall treble to bass string balance, and that seems to be good enough for this type of pickup.

20.10) Headstock Nut

Ready-to-go Necks

If you are re-using a known-good donor guitar neck, or using a reputable complete new "ready-to go" replacement neck, then you might proceed without any further worrying. All the fittings of the neck should be on it already, and hopefully, adjusted correctly. The nut string-slots might be higher than perfection, and thus more difficult to play, but should work reliably.

New Low-cost Necks

If you are buying a low-cost neck, or re-using a neck of unknown origin, be aware that there are a certain number of very low price necks on eBay. Some of the bargains are actually Asian factory rejects, because they each have one small inaccuracy in the manufacturing. If you can identify that inaccuracy, and fix it, you will get a very good neck, for a very small price. If you can not sort it out, then it will be second class. All the neck dimensions given throughout this book should help you diagnose any such neck manufacturing mistakes.

If you desire perfection, you might like to take a deep breath, then read on! The nut needs to be set, and maybe filed a little, such that every string is very close to, but never touching, the first fret. This ensures easy light-finger playing, with no unwanted string rattles.

Measure the string height action at the nut

I have an easy way to measure the nut height action by playing feel, to be used on each string: Place the guitar on it's back on a table, with the neck, as usual, on your left. Hold down the string onto the 5th fret with a right finger. Feel the height of play with a left finger on the first fret. It should be a very small, but clear definite, movement at the first fret.

Traditional nut cutting

The way guitars were made by hand, was to make the neck on the guitar, then shape the bone nut, and glue it on. String positions were then marked on, and string slots filed with a set of different string slot widths, using a specialist set of six nut files. Great care needed to be taken to get each slot, at the right angles, and down just enough, filed to exactly the right depth, to hold all the strings, very close to the frets, for easy playing.

The red-flag danger with this procedure, is that if you file the teensiest bit too far, that string will buzz horribly on the first or second fret. So, if you get into filing nut slots, be very patient, and frequently test the complete situation. Do this by playing the guitar, then measuring the string height above the first fret, near to the nut.

Ready-made nuts

Nowadays, it is possible to buy ready-made industry-standard S-Type nuts, which have accurate string slots already cut. This is my recommendation. They are usually 1/8in = 3.2mm thick. Most have a flat bottom, but some have a radius on the bottom, like the fret-board. Examine the shape of, and measure, the nut-slot that is on your neck, and buy a ready-made nut that fits it.

Test before glue

First test the nut on the neck, without any glue. The tension of the strings will hold it down temporarily. View the string slot heights by looking along the length of the neck from the heal. The frets should be all in-line and the bottom of the string slots should be just a teeny bit higher than the frets. Never lower than the frets. Test it properly by tuning the guitar and playing it. Measure the nut height action as I described above.

If the string slots are too high, take the nut off, and sand the bottom of the nut, flat and square, to reduce the height of the string slots. Replace the nut and re-test.

If the string slots are too low, you can pad the nut up a little bit with a small 1/8in = 3mm square shim under the nut at each end. The shim alone by itself will have temporary stability. When the nut is glued in, it will become long-term stable. The shims can be made of thick heavy paper, or very thin hard cardboard. Tack a shim at each end of the bottom of the nut slot with a drop of white glue. Insert the nut, tune up the strings, and test extensively.

When you are completely happy with the playing feel of the guitar, glue the nut into it's slot. Use white woodwork glue which is strong, but later removable. Do not use epoxy glue which is too strong, and very difficult to remove if you later want to replace the nut. Spread the white glue to cover all the bottom and both sides of the nut slot. Clean the surfaces of the nut, gently and quickly rubbing with P240 sandpaper. Insert the nut. Wipe off excess glue. Tension the strings to hold the nut down at the right height, while the glue dries.

Using nut files

On any guitar, you can reduce the height at the nut, of a string slot, by filing with a suitable sized nut slot file. Take great care to hold the file at the right angles while filing. The nut string slot should be straight in line with the long vibrating string.

The break angle is the angle between the long straight vibrating strings, and the short length of string, going back over the headstock, to the tuners or string trees. Hold the nut slot file at half of the break angle. This ensures that the string will thereafter sit comfortably, and reliably and evenly, on both the front edge, and the back edge, of the string slot. String tension should push down on both the front edge, and the back edge, of the perfect string slot.

Using a pen-knife

If you do not fancy the expense of various nut files, and you are making a small adjustment, you can chip away gently at the string slot with a pen-knife. Keep the string slot in line with the vibrating string. Keep the width not much wider than the string. Keep the bottom of the slot rounded, or a little bit V-shape. Keep the break angle correct, with the bottom of the slot flat, and at half the break angle. Jimmy Hendrix has been reported as often whittling at his nut slots with a pen-knife. However, I am sure he would have be delighted, if he were given a full set of expensive modern nut files!

Making a string slot higher

On any guitar, it is easy to make a string slot lower, but extremely difficult to make it reliably higher. You can clean a string slot with P240 sandpaper, re-fill it with epoxy or super-glue, and then re-shape the string slot. This works quite well, but does not last very long in my experience.

Replacing the nut

On any guitar, the best way to sort out a nut that is too low and rattly, on any string, is to replace the whole nut for a better one. It does not cost much. Although it sounds drastic, the procedure is easier than you might think, if you know how. Place the guitar flat on it's back on a table with a soft cloth. To cleanly remove an old nut, first cut it's thickness in half, using a hack-saw along the long width of the nut. That cut is about 43mm long. This splits the entire nut from 1/8in = 3.2mm thick, to two separated halves of 1.2mm thick. Take care to cut only through most of the full depth of the nut, and not touch the neck wood. Remove the two splits of the nut, off the wood, by firstly squeezing them together, with a pair of pliers, which breaks the glue joints cleanly. Then waggle the remaining half of the nut with the pliers. Clean up the slot. Re-start the nut fitting process with a new slotted nut. This time, do not let any nut string slots go too deep!

Roller nuts

On my expensive guitars, I use Fender LSR Roller nuts. They provide excellent tuning ease, and work snag-free, with a wide variety of string set weights. However, they require an unusual wider slot in the wood of the neck, and some wood-working precision in fitting. Once fitted, it is easy to refine the string heights up and down, several times, by placing the small stainless steel shims under the nut. The nut is fixed on with two small screws, into an accurate wide slot.

20.11) String Trees

String trees hold strings down as they pass over the nut and on to the tuners. This ensures that every string is in contact with the nut, both at the front, and the back of the nut, and that prevents buzzes and rattles.

String trees prevent the longer lengths of headstock string, from nut to tuner, from having their own vibrations. They would each, being of random length, be variously out of tune with the guitar.

Only the three top strings need a string tree. The three wound bass strings do not need, nor want, a string tree. It will only snag on the windings, and create tuning stutter. I make my own 3-string trees out of ertalyte, which is a strong low-friction, engineering plastic. In truth, any plastic would be nearly as good. If you use metal string trees, you must put a drop of oil on them, so that the strings slide nicely for stable tuning. If you can not find a 3-string tree, use two 2-string trees, and just unhook the wound D string, if that works better for easy tuning.

20.12) Happy Playing, and Maintenance

Your new guitar should now be ready to play extensively, and take out to gigs. Enjoy!

After a couple of months of use, check the string heights and the action. If you are using a new neck, and the string action has got higher, it is almost certainly because the neck truss rod has bedded into the neck wood a bit. That is due to the new constant tension, and probably will not happen again. The truss rod might need tightening slightly. See chapter 18.7)

The Next 500 Years

Whenever you put new strings on the guitar, lubricate each string with a small drop of oil, where it passes over, and hangs off the bridge piece, and where it passes under a string tree. This will facilitate smooth tuning. A tooth-pick is useful for placing each tiny drop of oil.

If your fretboard is a bare dark hardwood, give it a rub with lemon oil, or fretboard hydrate, with a small cotton rag, every six months, at a time that you are changing strings.

Clean the strings and neck of the guitar frequently with a microfibre cloth.

Buff up the body of the guitar once a year with a microfibre cloth.

If the body and neck needs cleaning, use a microfibre cloth dampened in very slightly soapy water, and rub gently.

If you have a high gloss finish, polish it after cleaning it. Use a guitar body care polish, or soft furniture polish, or just bees wax polish. Use a tiny bit of polish on a microfibre cloth, and rub extensively. Make sure that the cloth is perfectly clean, in order to not make new scratches with unwanted grit.

21) This Series of Guitars and Books

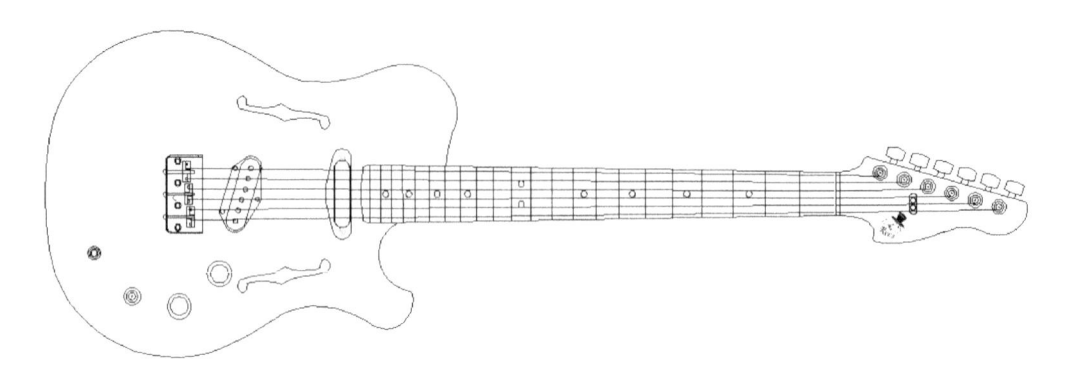

Available late 2020:
"How to Make Rees T-Style Semi-Acoustic Guitars"

All of the guitars in this series are designed on the same coordinate system. They have all the major parts at the same positions. You can easily make custom guitars, by mixing different necks, and bridges, and pickups, and controls.

Currently being written, Available 2021:
"How to Make Rees HH or P90 Semi-Acoustic Guitars"

22) Acknowledgements

Many thanks to all my friends and family, who have contributed to this project. It has been a lot more work than just writing another book of traditional guitar-making wisdom. New invention has required a huge amount of guitar testing by players. All that testing has refined and evaluated the guitars, in order to create and select the best designs that: sound greatest; play most expressively; and are very easy to make.

It has been a three year voyage of discovery, making, and modifying guitars, many times. These guys have helped throughout the project. About a dozen early-version guitars of various sizes, woods, and wood constructions have been assessed. The best of them, have been tried out at gigs with full bands, and modified in details.

Naturally, I did a lot of early testing of guitar prototypes. Then the professional guitarists did a lot of testing of the various final candidate guitars. They are: Ben Smith; Neil Cowlan; and Jimmy Brewer. They all tested some of the prototypes, and all of the final guitars, in acoustic and electric modes, in a wide variety of playing styles. They performed gigs with them, and recorded with them. Their feedback has greatly contributed to the quality of these guitars. They all helped raise the final standard of the design from "best amateur guitar" to "best professional guitar".

Professor Jim Woodhouse of The University of Cambridge Engineering Department. Jim gave me several important tips on how to analyse the resonance modes of stringed acoustic musical instrument soundboards. His knowledge helped me extend the bass response of these semi-acoustic guitars.

Dr John Nuttall, who tested the prototype book by reading only it, and making his first ever self-built guitar. He did that successfully, and without any significant help from me, other than the book! Feedback from John has enhanced the quality, and detailed accuracy, of this series of books.

My dear wife Vicenta, who tolerated guitar building in our small garden, when I had to retreat to home from my large workshop, during the 2020 government work-at-home directive.

Website links:

Ben Smith: www.bensmithguitar.com
Neil Cowlan: www.neilcowlan.com
Jimmy Brewer: www.smithandbrewer.com
Clive Rees: www.rees-electric-guitars.com
Latest Support Information: www.rees-electric-guitars.com

End of this book.
Beginning of your fine new guitar. Enjoy!

Printed in Great Britain
by Amazon